JUN   2009

338.54?
Depres
Nelsor
33341(

Depression

2.0

WITHDRAWN

JUN 2003

Depression 2.0

CREATIVE STRATEGIES FOR TOUGH ECONOMIC TIMES

BY CLETUS NELSON

2.0

Alameda Free Library
1550 Oak Street
Alameda, CA 94501

process self-reliance series

Depression 2.0 © 2009 by Cletus Nelson and Process Media

Depression 2.0 is the fourth volume in the Process Self-Reliance Series

**Preparedness Now! An Emergency Survival Guide
for Civilians and Their Families**
by Aton Edwards
ISBN 978-0976082255

Getting Out: Your Guide to Leaving America
by Mark Ehrman
ISBN 978-0976082279

**The Urban Homestead: Your Guide to
Self-Sufficient Living in the Heart of the City**
by Kelly Coyne and Erik Knutzen
ISBN 978-1934170014

Process Media
1240 W. Sims Way #124
Port Townsend, WA 98368

www.processmediainc.com

ISBN 978-1934170069

10 9 8 7 6 5 4 3 2 1

Table of Contents

Chapter 1

INTRODUCTION
THE RECKONING

Introduction: The Reckoning

IT'S HARD NOT TO LOOK BACK ON THE LAST FEW YEARS WITHOUT A sense of deep regret. As both a nation and a people, we've maxed out our credit cards, mortgaged ourselves to the hilt and never quite gotten around to saving any money. And there was no shortage of willing enablers. When our mailboxes weren't stuffed with credit card offers, shady mortgage brokers were cold-calling us at dinnertime offering us six-figure loans with no money down, or a tantalizing home equity line of credit to fuel the next spending spree. In this gilded, get-it-now atmosphere, recessions were never an option; Wall Street bankers could always count on the Federal Reserve to open up the money spigots and keep the party going. In Washington, DC, our free-spending politicians convinced themselves that deficits needn't matter when there's a friendly overseas lender just a phone call away. In short, we've been living beyond our means for far too long, and now the bubble has burst. This book concerns itself with how we can cope with the painful national hangover that we can call Depression 2.0.

As we contemplate the future in this age of nail-biting uncertainty, perhaps out greatest challenges will be psychological in nature. Do we have the necessary mental toughness to persevere in the face of severe economic setbacks? Can we retain our sense of optimism when the nation is drowning in a sea of red ink? We've spent our entire lives living in a stable, prosperous consumer paradise, and it's all we've ever known. Do we possess the necessary resolve and determination that allowed our forebears to weather the privations of the Great Depression? Only time will tell. However, it is sincerely hoped that the present work will offer a positive step in the right direction by providing consumers with a valuable guidebook for these perilous economic times.

Practical and common sense strategies for surviving on less in an age of diminishing expectations are provided in the following pages. The current difficulties—though they do present formidable challenges—needn't be cause for fear, pessimism or despair. The crucible of adversity brings communities closer together, and can unleash our creative powers in ways we never thought possible. By and large, Americans are an optimistic, free-spirited and innovative people. These enduring qualities will play an important role in how we move forward from Depression 2.0.

Our nation is at a crossroads. Every facet of our existence—how and where we live, what we eat, where we work and even what forms of transportation we use—could be undergoing a seismic shift in the near future. While economic circumstances will certainly play a role in altering our present lifestyles, many of these changes may simply be inevitable. The looming threat of global warming, resource scarcity, a crumbling national infrastructure and a dysfunctional political culture may force us to part ways with the status quo and look for alternatives. It is highly likely that many of these innovations will occur on a local or community level as citizens start working together to find solutions to the problems we face.

Those who are adequately prepared and able to seamlessly make the transition to a more sustainable way of living will have a decisive advantage. It is hoped that this book will provide the necessary knowledge, guidance and inspiration to those seeking to adapt to our present circumstances. In the popular mind, living with less means a life of near-constant misery and perpetual want. However, a satisfying, purposeful life needn't be shackled to the bottom line. Above all else, hopefully this book will foster a spirit of free-wheeling experimentation. While each of us will likely experience numerous false starts and missteps on the road to self-sufficiency, every setback has the potential to plant the seeds of future successes.

So, how exactly did our supercharged economy go off the rails? This question is of no small significance. Many Americans have been completely taken aback by the sheer magnitude of the current financial crisis. Yet there were already a number of ominous signs indicating that we were treading on thin ice. Unfortunately, we made the mistake of trusting our financial and governmental institutions to responsibly safeguard our nation's wealth. This isn't an option anymore. Each of us needs to take the time to become better informed about economic matters. Perhaps it is well worth our time to briefly examine the roots of the current crisis, and illuminate a couple of dangerous trends that could impact our financial future.

The Dollar in Decline

THE SIGNING OF THE BRETTON WOODS AGREEMENTS, IN JULY 1944, was a pivotal moment in U.S. economic history. The historic accords would allow the dollar to play a uniquely influential role in the postwar economic order. The majority of the world's currencies would be pegged to the dollar, and U.S. currency would become the preferred medium of exchange for key commodities like oil, natural gas and precious metals. The dollar would become indispensable to the world economy. Moreover, every dollar in circulation at that time was backed by a percentage of the nation's formidable gold reserves held inside the legendary Fort Knox Bullion Depository in Northern Kentucky. One fateful decision changed all that.

In 1971, the Nixon administration was facing growing opposition to the Vietnam conflict. Sensing the public mood, a stubborn Congress refused to appropriate additional funding for the war, and a tax hike was simply out of the question. Desperate to carry out his policies in Vietnam, Nixon borrowed the money to continue the war. A spending spree ensued, and billions of dollars were injected into the economy, resulting in severe inflation. Hoping to head off a crisis, Nixon instituted wage and price freezes, implemented a tax on imports and, with one stroke of the presidential pen, took the U.S. off the gold standard. "This move ended the era of stability," explains currency historian Jack Weatherford, "and the period of greatest economic prosperity and productivity in the history of the American dollar."[1]

It truly was the end of an era. The Bretton Woods agreements were thrown into disarray, and the once-mighty greenback was transformed from a value-based "hard" currency that enjoyed the supreme confidence of international investors to a "fiat" or "floating" currency. The dollar was now backed by little more than consumer faith and U.S. government promises. "Before anyone fully realized how it happened," recounts Weatherford, "the dollar was on a roller coaster, but the Japanese yen and the German mark seemed to be on an ever-upward track, while the dollar fluctuated in the short run but fell in the long run."[2]

Obviously there would be both winners and losers when Nixon fatefully severed the link between the dollar and the nation's gold reserves. As the dollar's precipitous fall spread through the world economy, currencies in Bolivia and Peru, which were pegged to the once rock-solid dollar, proved unable to withstand the wild fluctuations and crashed. American consumers would be hobbled with a constantly rising cost of living and diminished buying power; the same dollar that could buy 1/35 of an ounce of gold in 1970 buys less than 1/800 of an ounce today. However, politicians, government officials and well-connected business interests would reap huge benefits from the fiat currency system.

When a currency operates under a gold standard, governments can only spend what is backed by a percentage of the nation's gold reserves. By contrast, a floating currency is the equivalent of a moneymaking machine to cash-hungry government officials and politicians. Once the U.S. dropped the gold standard, the nation embarked on a spending spree unmatched in human history. A vast overseas empire, gargantuan defense budgets, farm subsidies, corporate stimulus packages and myriad other spending initiatives drove the national debt to record heights.

However, runaway government spending was only part of the problem. When there is greater political control over a given currency system, the temptation to tinker with the economy is all too often the result. The Federal Reserve system, formed in the aftermath of the historic 1907 liquidity crisis, was instituted in 1913 to oversee the nation's banking system, maintain an elastic currency and ensure price stability. However, in recent years, the Fed has become an altogether different animal.

Because the Federal Reserve controls the money supply, our nation's central bankers have a powerful tool at their disposal. When the Fed slashes interest rates or buys dollar-denominated securities on the open market, these actions increase the number of dollars in circulation and can provide an artificial, short-term boost to the economy. While these types of interventions may have helped us avoid recessions in the recent past, they come at a very high cost by diluting the dollar and eroding our purchasing power. Indeed, the dollar's declining value when compared to the Euro is but one indication of how the Federal Reserve's recent activities have impacted the lives of consumers.

While the more optimistic will argue that an artificially weakened dollar lowers the price of U.S. goods and spurs international trade, America's unproductive economy has shown few signs of capitalizing on this opportunity. Instead, we import hundreds of billions of dollars more than we export overseas. This is known as our "current account" deficit, and when we suffer from this type of trade imbalance, we are forced to borrow money from foreign lenders to make up the difference.

Between our $10 trillion national debt and growing current account deficit, which runs into the hundreds of billions, we have now become reliant on the largesse of foreign lenders like China, Japan and various oil-rich Gulf states to maintain our way of life. In 2008, James Fallows reported in the *Atlantic Monthly* that "Every person in the (rich) United States has over the past ten years or so borrowed about $4,000 from someone in the (poor) People's

Republic of China."[3] Yet this cannot go on indefinitely. The dollar's status as the world's reserve currency has bought us some time, but at some point the rest of the world might decide that they can no longer bet on the productive capacity of the U.S. economy or our ability to pay off our monumental debts, and start jettisoning dollar holdings.

The precarious position of the dollar also leaves us uniquely vulnerable to economic warfare. Indeed, there is already historical precedent for such a strategy. During the 1956 Suez Crisis, President Eisenhower pressured the British into withdrawing from their campaign against Egypt by threatening to dump America's pound holdings onto the open market, which would have precipitated a British currency crisis.

The U.S. could find itself in a similar situation should the oil-producing nations insist that the Euro replace the dollar as the dominant currency for all petroleum transactions. Should this come to pass, the rest of the world would have little reason to maintain stockpiles of U.S. currency that could drastically devalue the dollar. China has also amassed a significant stockpile of dollar-denominated securities that could severely undermine the U.S. economy should its leaders decide to exercise what is called "the nuclear option" and unload these sizeable holdings.

Like many fiat currencies throughout history, the dollar has long since lost its primary role as an effective medium of exchange. When our money became a theoretical plaything for economic central planners and a political instrument for politicians, the economic realities of the average consumer ceased to be a concern. The cost of a mismanaged currency isn't just the "stealth tax" we pay each year when our dollars buy less and our cost of living rises. Indeed, as we shall see in the next section, the Federal Reserve's currency policies are at least partially responsible for the current economic crisis.

Anatomy of a Meltdown

BACK IN 1995, WHEN MOST OF US WERE FIRST SURFING THE WEB USING primitive dial-up modems, then-Federal Reserve Chairman Alan Greenspan believed he'd seen the future. In his mind's eye, the revolutionary potential of computer technology was destined to usher in a new economic era. "When historians look back on the latter half of the 1990s," he would later remark, "I suspect that they will conclude that we are now living through a pivotal period in American economic history."[4]

Pivotal it was, but perhaps not in the way that the once-celebrated Fed Chief intended. However, the ever-optimistic monetary expert was not to be denied his vision. Indeed, for a while it seemed like he was on to some-

CHARLES HUGH SMITH ON
THE POST-CONSUMER SOCIETY

Charles Hugh Smith is an entrepreneur, financial commentator, and
the author of seven books. Smith's insightful musings on critical
financial and economic issues can be found on his popular
website/blog *www.oftwominds.com*.

....

Q: *You've advised your readers to avoid the "distraction" of inflationary and
deflationary trends and pay closer attention to purchasing power. Are there
any practical ways we can get more bang for our buck?*

CHS: Definitely. The problem with trying to reckon "deflation" and "inflation"
is that the answer depends on what's being measured—assets, currency, commodities, etc.—and in what time frame. Was oil shooting from $60 to $147
deflationary or inflationary? How about when it dropped from $147 to $35?
The deflation-inflation debate offers little practical help.

The key to maintaining purchasing power is to accept that high volatility
will continue across assets, currencies and commodities, and the nimble and
flexible will likely do much better than those seeking one "answer." In such
an environment, it's practical to view all purchases and investments as hedges
against future unknowns. For example, gold is a hedge against all paper currencies dropping in purchasing power, and hence its popularity as one more-or-less
sure way of retaining purchasing power vis-à-vis paper currencies.

Some feel that there is no substitute for owning physical gold, while others
who recall that the federal government appropriated all private physical gold in
the 1930s prefer to own gold held elsewhere (such as Switzerland), via companies such as BullionVault.

thing. His message of constant growth and increased productivity coincided perfectly with the rise of the Internet and the advent of Silicon Valley as a nexus of American innovation. As talk of the "New Economy" spread, the public was duly informed that the brick-and-mortar businesses of the past were on the verge of being replaced by a vast array of lucrative technological products and services that would power the U.S. economy for years to come and transform the world.

Taking a cue from the visionary Fed Chairman, bullish investors went on a sustained buying binge. Soon, dozens of companies, many of which had yet to earn a profit, were financed with billions from speculators looking to cash in on "the next big thing." Internet-savvy baby boomers seeking a solid investment portfolio for their retirement years quickly jumped on board, and the sheer influx of cash drove the stock market to record heights. The Dow Jones Industrial Average, which was under 4,000 in 1994, would catapult to over 11,000 in just a few short years.[5] The NASDAQ would enjoy a similar rise, bounding from 500 to 6000 in the overheated 1990s.[6]

Greenspan would play a key role in the ensuing boom, repeatedly cutting interest rates to fuel the non-stop feeding frenzy. As skeptical investors began to question the surging stock prices, he defended the higher valuations on the basis of his belief in America's newfound productivity. When Long Term Capital Management, a billion-dollar hedge fund, failed in 1998, and the market began to cool, the Fed Chief stepped in with yet another cut in interest rates to keep the easy credit flowing. These efforts, according to author William Fleckenstein, "came to be viewed as the 'Greenspan Put,' meaning speculators could take enormous amounts of risk trusting that Greenspan would do anything to stop the market from a serious decline."[7]

However, as the millennium dawned, the signs of a speculative bubble (excess liquidity, overvalued stock) were there for all to see. By February 2000, the fast and furious stock trading was reaching dangerous levels. By that time, margin debt, which is money loaned by brokers to cover a percentage of stock purchases, exceeded $265 billion.[8] As margin debt is one of the leading indicators of a speculative bubble, the crash wasn't long in coming. By the middle of March 2000, stocks began heading south. Over the next two years, some $5 trillion in paper profits would be effectively wiped out.

The huge productivity gains envisioned by Greenspan and his starry-eyed acolytes never materialized. While the '90s was a decade of impressive innovation, and a commendable uptick in corporate performance, there was little evidence of the revolutionary gains predicting by Greenspan. In the meantime, trillions of dollars that could have been invested in more sustainable, productive ventures was funneled down the dot.com sinkhole. By 2001, the economy

But the essential commodities—oil, grain and other food—can fluctuate wildly even if priced in gold. Thus it makes sense to buy the essentials of life such as food and energy when prices are low (in terms of dollars or gold), as a hedge against future higher prices. Oil can be traded via futures contracts or ETFs like XLE or OIL, or via oil/natural gas/exploration/refining companies.

Volatile markets in currencies and essential commodities make for a very difficult environment. The owner of dollars might be losing, but the holder of dollars invested in oil/energy stocks might be beating the holder of gold. The person with a hundred pounds of rice and fifty pounds of dried beans on hand will at least be hedged against temporary food shortages.

Q: *In the future, you believe consumers are more likely to view housing as simply a form of shelter as opposed to a long-term investment. In the interim, do you see co-housing arrangements, eco-villages, micro-homes and other alternatives emerging as a free market response to outsized rents and mortgages?*

CHS: Absolutely. One theme I have addressed repeatedly is the reversal of housing density—the trend toward one person, one dwelling shifting back to multi-person households. The reason is obvious: The cost of housing in the U.S. is very high compared to a generation or two ago, as measured by "hours of labor needed to rent an apartment." As Depression 2.0 takes hold, incomes will shrink or disappear and people will move to cheaper or free lodging. Choices include moving in with family members who own a dwelling that's free and clear (some twenty-five million homes have no mortgage), renting one of the millions of spare bedrooms that will be available for rent/trade (perhaps elderly homeowners will be trading shelter for help with chores/meal prep, etc.) or occupying (i.e., squatting) some of the eighteen million unoccupied dwellings in the U.S.

began to falter and a long overdue hangover from the excesses of the 1990s drove the market toward a recession.

At this juncture the public had long grown wary of investing in the stock market. Yet suddenly a new opportunity arose. All that residual dot.com wealth and a new trend in subprime home mortgages led to a white-hot real estate market. Once again, Greenspan acted as head cheerleader for the ensuing bubble by cutting interest rates below two percent and publicly touting the new opportunities available to homeowners. By 2004, consumers had amassed nearly $7 trillion in mortgage debt as popular home equity loans and question-able subprime mortgages kept the flagging economy going.[9]

Innovations in finance allowed the majority of America's consumer mort-gages to be bundled and repackaged as tradable securities. As the demand for these newly minted bond offerings escalated, the system began to break down. Brokers were pressured to increase the number of home loans in circulation to fuel the traffic in mortgage-backed securities. Soon the loan approval process became little more than a formality. Consumers with little collateral and poor credit histories could apply online for lucrative loans and get approved within minutes.

The excess liquidity pushed home prices to unsustainable heights. Yet this was only part of the problem. Wall Street's self-professed "Masters of the Universe" began wildly trafficking in mortgage-backed securities and using these dubious assets as collateral to leverage their sizeable financial specula-tions. As these "off-balance-sheet" holdings mounted, there were insufficient controls in place to gauge the risks the firms were taking on. The advent of credit default swaps, a type of derivative that acts as a form of insurance if a given financial institution can't cover its trading positions, only further compli-cated the picture and hastened the ensuing meltdown when an epidemic of mortgage defaults in 2007–08 left our nation's most revered investment banks and institutions holding trillions in worthless paper and unable to cover their debts. As the ensuing crisis spread, the world's credit system was plunged into an unprecedented crisis that has now spread throughout the economy.

This tragic destruction of our nation's wealth offers a sobering reminder that even our most respected financial experts and Ivy League economists can fall victim to the kind of delusional groupthink we often ascribe to millenarian religious sects and exotic cargo cults. The mass psychosis that fueled both the dot.com boom and the housing bubble both rested on the groundless assumption that stock prices and home values were on a permanent upward track, and that recessions were a relic of the past. Yet the most fatal conceit of all was the widely-held belief that there was relative safety in wagering trillions of dollars that consumers wouldn't default on their mortgages.

Having written about the co-housing movement since 1991, I see it as a model for group housing which offers a lifestyle that is far superior to living alone. Co-housing requires a serious investment of time and cooperation, which depends on trustworthy communication, completing tasks as assigned/agreed on and tolerance/listening skills. The payoffs are increased security and community—two assets of increasing value in hard times.

It's entirely possible that we will see heretofore unimaginable living arrangements, such as defunct mini-malls being taken over by co-ops and the retail spaces being used as residential lofts. The key will be proximity to services and functioning communities and the energy required to heat and light the spaces. Malls in the middle of nowhere may well be bulldozed as nuisances, if counties can spare the diesel fuel for the dozers.

Ironically, the best way to "look out for number one" will be to start looking out for numbers two through ten—those who share your neighborhood, house or community.

Q: *In your blog posts and commentaries, you emphasize that there is every reason to be optimistic about the future. What, in your opinion, are the positive benefits of living in a post-consumer society?*

CHS: As commentator/author Richard Metzger has noted, one of the biggest positives will be the reduction in stress. People assume the high-stress rat race they currently survive with anti-anxiety pills and other drugs is somehow easier than what they call "poverty." But beyond shelter, electricity and basic healthy food, the real poverty is in the lives of those working soulless jobs to make enough money to pay for their SUV, ski trips charged on credit cards, low-quality furniture and gadgetry, bloated, energy-wasting McMansions and distracting electronics. Poverty as experienced in the third world—shelterless hunger—is somewhat unlikely in the U.S., which retains a wealth of agricultural resources, some oil/energy and eighteen million empty dwellings, but the "poverty" of no longer being able to afford the distractions of middle-class life may actually enhance people's lives.

It will likely take years to restore the nation's financial equilibrium after the excesses of the last few years, and history will not be kind to Alan Greenspan or his deluded flock. Unfortunately, we can't hit the reset button; the damage has already been done. While it is hoped that we are witnessing the dawning of a new era characterized by responsible investing, greater regulatory oversight and advanced risk management systems, if history is any guide, we needn't get our hopes up. In a few short years, we can be certain that Wall Street's best and brightest will begin marching in lockstep heralding the arrival of the "next big thing," and the cycle will begin anew.

The Entitlement Time Bomb

IF THE SUCCESSIVE DEBACLES THAT HAVE PLAGUED THE FINANCIAL world have greatly imperiled our nation's economic future, our elected representatives have added to our difficulties. The profligate spending that has pushed our national debt to over $10 trillion is just the tip of the iceberg. On January 1, 2011, the picture grows even darker. On that portentous date, the first members of America's baby boom generation will be eligible for retirement benefits, possibly unleashing a tidal wave of government debt that could send shudders through the U.S. economy for years to come.

At issue are two highly problematic government entitlement programs: Medicare and Social Security. The latter operates on what is called a pay-as-you-go basis; each year, payroll deductions from current employees and their employers are redirected toward retirees. Once these expenditures have been allocated, the remaining revenues are placed in the Social Security Trust Fund. However, this poses a major problem: Baby boomers are the biggest generation in the history of the U.S. In other words, there may not be enough people working and paying into the system to keep the Trust Fund solvent once the mass retirement begins. Although there is no exact date, sometime within the next few decades the Social Security Administration (SSA) will begin hemorrhaging cash and start drawing down the Trust Fund. When this day dawns, we will quickly learn that despite all the promises we often hear about the sanctity of our nation's retirement funds, our politicians have been raiding the till for years.

The federal government has run sizeable budget deficits for thirty-five of the last forty years. In the hopes of disguising these debts and covering expenses, our myopic elected officials have been siphoning money from the Social Security Fund like a degenerate gambler at a casino ATM machine. In less than ten years, 2017 to be exact, the government will begin paying out more in Social Security benefits than it takes in, and that's when the real

No more cable or satellite TV? That's an instant improvement in sanity and well-being. No more fat and sugar-loaded snacks and fast foods? Ditto. Self-reliance has a number of rewards—rewards those of us who baked bread and fixed our own bikes and cars in the late '60s/early '70s experienced firsthand. Home-cooked food is cheaper, better for you and tastes much better than greasy fast foods, for example—once a person is weaned by "poverty" from high-salt, high-fat, high-sugar packaged and fast food.

People will have more free time in "poverty," and they will then have the opportunity to do all the "good, creative things" they could never do when on the treadmill of middle-class "wealth."

Some of my readers criticize what they see as a moralistic pleasure in the decline of the so-called "comforts" of middle-class American life, but I believe it is merely practical. Being overweight, addicted to pills/painkillers, eating wretched "food" you wouldn't in good conscience feed your pet, addicted to mindless, destructive videogames and TV and unable to do much for yourself in the real world does not seem appealing, regardless of "wealth" or income.

Q: *You're strongly critical of fiat currencies as a medium of exchange. Do you see community currencies or a sophisticated barter system playing a greater role in American life?*

CHS: I see the potential for local "scripts," bartering currencies and international trading currencies based on either gold or on a basket of commodities such as oil and gold. In other words, we may see parallel systems rise alongside the current fiat national currencies.

Locally, there are already movements afoot in the U.S. to establish "scripts" that can be earned and traded for regional goods and services; while I am no expert, others see these as legal arrangements because the script is not currency.

Internationally, the gold ETF (exchange-traded fund) GLD probably has enough gold in its vaults to back an international trading currency, which could be used for transactions in which dollars (or any other paper currency) are no longer desired. In other words, the commercial interests of the global economy might establish a completely private currency for trading purposes.

trouble begins. Congress won't be able to tap the Fund to cover expenses, which will result in additional public spending, increased deficits and a greater percentage of our gross domestic product (GDP) allocated toward servicing our nation's mounting debts. Moreover, by the time that Generation X gets ready to retire, the Trust Fund may be exhausted.

Medicare, another program for retirees, is in even worse shape. The health insurance program is primarily funded through payroll deductions and insurance premiums, with the remaining revenue socked away in a trust fund. However, the skyrocketing health care costs of current retirees, massive fraud and other problems are pushing the program to the brink of insolvency. The program is currently paying out more in benefits than it takes in revenues, and the Medicare Trust Fund is expected to be exhausted as early as 2019—but this could come even sooner due to shrinking tax revenues and other complications.[10]

Although expert estimates vary, at the very least we can expect an overall debt burden somewhere in the ballpark of $50 trillion to cover projected future retirement outlays.[11] Obviously the impending retirement crisis will pose a difficult challenge to a cash-strapped nation and the clock is already ticking. While there may still be time for reform, if we don't act soon, we may be sleepwalking into a period of severe economic instability characterized by massive government debt, exorbitant levels of taxation and a lowered standard of living. When the government is harnessed by debt, a reduction in critical services may also become a serious consideration. One must also keep in mind that America's economic standing will become that much more vulnerable to any sort of economic shock like war, severe natural disasters or serious fuel shortage.

The Oil Dilemma

OIL HAS OFTEN BEEN LIKENED TO OXYGEN: WE DON'T GIVE IT MUCH thought until the supply starts to run out. When oil prices soar, it seems difficult to ignore how much of modern life is directly linked to cheap and abundant fuel. We don't just burn it up driving on the freeway; an estimated 90% of all organic chemicals we use—like plastics, pharmaceuticals and fertilizers—are derived from petroleum.[12] Even the food we eat requires large amounts of fuel now that modern agriculture has become increasingly reliant on fossil fuels in order to run irrigation systems, for pesticides, and for shipping crops to market. For this reason, the belief that the world's largest oil fields are becoming dangerously depleted has become a serious cause for concern.

There is only a finite amount of oil we can extract from the earth—roughly two trillion barrels—and our problems will truly begin when the industrialized

CHARLES HUGH SMITH continued

There are also moves to create regional currencies in Asia and the Arabian Gulf that might be backed by a basket of commodities. Any of these currencies, if truly backed by oil or gold, would quickly find favor among those seeking to retain the purchasing power of their assets.

There is no reason such transnational currencies couldn't find favor locally as well. We might even see three prices for desirable goods: one in dollars, one in local script and one in quatloos (a gold or oil-backed currency).

Q: *We are often told that consumer spending is the only way we can keep the economy afloat and maintain our current standard of living. What would transpire if millions of Americans were to tear up their credit cards?*

CHS: In essence, that is what we're seeing. People are sensing that they will have to rely at least partially on their own means rather than count on government to provide pensions and health care. The reduction in debt and debt-fueled spending is re-ordering the economy—in terms of shrinking the economy, we call it a depression. But a shrinking GDP is not necessarily a destruction of happiness if we re-order the economy.

Ideally, we will replace an oil-dependent, exporting financial "instruments," importing cheap-goods consumerist economy with one that spends $10 trillion or so replacing the oil-energy complex with a new energy-efficient, non-fossil fuel economy. Abundant, reasonable-cost energy will make all sorts of other problems easier to resolve. High-cost, shortage-prone energy will make solving all the other problems more or less impossible.

When oil is $30/barrel, few see a need for a new energy economy; when it's $300/barrel, everyone will be wondering why we waited until the last minute to take concerted action.

Q: *Peak Oil remains a subject of contentious debate. Do you see any sort of consensus emerging anytime soon?*

world has reached the halfway point, or what is called "Peak Oil." If we look upon global oil production as a bell curve, when we reach the peak or mid-point, the amount of available oil will begin to diminish with each passing year. Moreover, production will become more costly and difficult as existing reserves become exhausted and the crude becomes more difficult to extract from the earth.

There are severe economic consequences to such a development. Peak Oil theorists, who believe that we will reach this crisis point sometime within this decade, predict that gasoline would top $8 a gallon and that food short-ages could ensue, because of disrupted supply chains and a shortage of petroleum-based fertilizers. The market for inexpensive imports from China and Japan would vanish due to increased shipping costs, and some of the more pessimistic even believe that U.S. cities in locations that experience extreme weather conditions could become uninhabitable due to exorbitant heating or cooling costs.

Peak Oil theory is based on the predictions of the late M. King Hubbert, a Shell Oil geophysicist and world-renowned authority on the world's petroleum reserves. In the mid-1950s, the native Texan trained his formidable intellect on a single goal: determining the production capacity of America's oil fields. Deploying the time-tested methods of population biologists, who measure how populations affect the sustainability of natural resources, along with a mathematical model based on existing oil reserves and the average rates of production and consumption, Hubbert detected a distinct downward trend in how oil is extracted from the earth. At first production flows smoothly and then, over time, it peaks, and production rates slow down until existing sup-plies are exhausted.

Although he was initially ridiculed for his 1956 prediction that U.S. oil production would begin declining after 1970, Hubbert's estimates proved to be uncannily accurate. During the Nixon era, American oil companies topped out at over nine million barrels per day, and American oil extraction has been in decline ever since. Hubbert's methods (and other measures) have been applied to the world's existing oil fields by a new generation of scientists. While we have yet to see a serious consensus, a number of experts are growing con-cerned that the Age of Oil could be entering its final climactic stage.

This is not to say that there aren't skeptics. Some geologists base their estimates on the total amount of oil currently in the ground divided by the rate of consumption, which is known as the Reserves to Production or "R/P" ratio. Using this method, it is believed that industrial societies will enjoy an additional forty to a hundred years of available oil. Peak Oil detractors also point out that advanced technological methods for extracting oil, the growth and evolution of alternative fuels, and various changes in human behavior may

CHS: Yes—when depletion of the supergiant fields in Mexico, Saudi Arabia and elsewhere finally lower supply irrevocably below demand. That moment when denial ends and consensus solidifies will occur once the recent spate of new production ceases adding new supply to offset the declines in the super-giant fields which supply about half the world's oil.

Then denialists will pin all their hopes on natural gas, but that has the same depletion curve as oil—as do coal and uranium, dashing the hopes of those pinning all their hopes for cheap and abundant energy on gas, coal or nuclear power. There will certainly be roles for fossil fuels and nuclear power in the future, but the era of cheap, abundant oil is over, and the era of cheap, abundant natural gas and coal is also ending. Once oil and its equivalents cost $300/barrel in today's dollars, then the alternatives will look cheap.

Many poorly-informed pundits are fond of extolling North America's unlimited shale oil and tar sands, but a little research reveals that these require staggering amounts of natural gas and water to process, and they leave hundreds of square miles of wasteland in their wake. Even worse, experts suggest that these "alternative fossil fuels" will top out at about three million barrels a day in actual practical terms—about 15% of the twenty million barrels of oil the U.S. consumes each day. The real "pie in the sky" energy source isn't solar energy—it's shale oil and tar sands.

The problem is that scaling up alternatives and making our society energy-efficient will cost a stupendous amount of money. If we're spending much of our capital buying oil for $300/barrel, then there is that much less capital available to construct an alternative energy complex.

The sad irony is the consensus on Peak Oil will finally form after it's too late to replace it without major sacrifices. •

alter the inexorable and often doom-laden Peak Oil hypothesis. Economists also point out that once oil becomes too costly, there will be financial incentives to devise alternatives that will forestall any serious crisis.

Unfortunately, the transition won't happen overnight. MIT geologist David Goodstein believes it will take "years, perhaps decades to replace the vast infrastructure, distribution and consumption of the products of the twenty billion barrels of oil we Americans alone gobble up each day."[13] Meanwhile, America is also being outflanked by rising nations like China in the worldwide scramble to exploit the world's petroleum reserves. Moreover, oil-producing nations that oppose U.S. policies—like Russia, Iran, Venezuela and others—are making overtures to fuel-thirsty rising economic powers like China and India in the hopes of limiting American influence among the world's oil-producing nations.

The volatility of oil markets, instability caused by America's diminishing role among oil-producing nations and the possible onset of Peak Oil could greatly impact American economic life in the immediate future. The modern economy has long been based on the assumption that inexpensive oil will long remain the prevailing norm. Moreover, when we take into account the looming issue of global warming, a radical change in our current energy policy seems inevitable. Whether the scenario envisioned by Peak Oil theorists is a certainty or a rough draft of the future depends on many variables that are difficult to predict. However, we can be certain that the issue of energy dependence will profoundly impact the American economy for years to come.

Entering the Unknown

WHAT WE HAVE RECOUNTED ABOVE ARE THE PRIMARY SYMPTOMS OF Depression 2.0: a woefully mismanaged currency, runaway government spending, real estate and financial markets debilitated by speculative excess, and a slow-motion energy crisis. Nevertheless, it is well worth keeping in mind that people have been predicting the untimely demise of the U.S. economy for a number of years, yet the American marketplace possesses an almost supernatural resilience. While it is tempting to make comparisons with the Great Depression of the early 20th century, it is worth bearing in mind that we may have a decisive advantage over our 1930s counterparts.

The Americans of the early 20th century didn't possess the tools we have at our fingertips. Today it is far easier to start a business, sell a product, market a new invention or merely solicit assistance than it was over half a century ago. The advent of the internet and the many social networking programs available are valuable assets that will prove vital to us in the immediate future. However, this is not to say that we can't learn an important lesson from America's greatest generation. As the Great Depression took its toll, and millions of Americans faced unprecedented poverty, many communities across the country mobilized and worked together forming barter networks, giving to charity, volunteering or simply helping out neighbors in need. This admirable tradition will play an important role in surmounting the difficulties of Depression 2.0. •

Notes

1   Weatherford, Jack. *The History of Money*, (New York: Three Rivers, 1997), p. 185.

2   Ibid., p. 186.

3   Fallows, James. "The $1.4 Trillion Question," *Atlantic Monthly*, January/February 2008.

4   Congressional Testimony, March 6, 2000.

5   Morgenson, Gretchen. "Dow Surpasses 11,000 as Base of Rally Grows," *New York Times*, May 4, 1999.

6   Kelleher, Kevin. "Flashing Back to NASDAQ 5000," TheStreet.com, March 10, 2005.

7   Fleckenstein, William A. *Greenspan's Bubbles: The Age of Ignorance at the Federal Reserve*, (New York: McGraw-Hill, 2008), p. 55.

8   Ibid., p. 87.

9   Hagenbaugh, Barbara. "Consumer Debt Loads At Record," *USA Today*, March 17, 2004.

10 Freking, Kevin. "Economy Likely to Move Up Medicare's Insolvency," Associated Press, December 1, 2008.

11 Muhleisen, Martin and Christopher Towe, (eds.) U.S. Fiscal Policies and Priorities for Long-Run Sustainability, International Monetary Fund (IMF) Publications, January 7, 2004.

12 Goodstein, David. *Out of Gas: The End of the Age of Oil*, (New York: W.W. Norton & Company, 2004), p. 15.

13 Ibid., p. 18.

CHAPTER 2

WORST CASE SCENARIO

CONTEMPLATING UNEMPLOYMENT

Worst Case Scenario:
Contemplating Unemployment

YOUR ORDEAL MIGHT BEGIN WITH A FRIENDLY E-MAIL FROM YOUR human resources department. Perhaps management would like a list of your official duties and some helpful recommendations. Who could take on some of your job responsibilities if you were "on vacation" or "out sick"? You can be certain these questions will be asked with the utmost tact and sensitivity. Nevertheless, the unspoken message will be difficult to ignore: someone may be deciding whether your job is expendable. Sometimes the warning signs can be a bit subtler. You might notice a lot of closed-door meetings among the senior staff, or your project manager might have become strangely distant over the last few weeks. While you might survive the first round of cuts, if there's another ritual bloodletting, you may not be so lucky.

Unless you're an elected official, a Supreme Court Justice or your dad just happens to own the company, job security becomes a precious commodity when the economy is in crisis. When companies struggle with thinning (or non-existent) profits, reducing overhead is often the first line of defense. This usually means downsizing existing staff—and that's where you come in. If you're one of the fortunate ones and are still hanging on to your current position, don't make the mistake of growing complacent. Sweeping staff cuts could be just around the corner. Since you have a bit of breathing room, now is the perfect time to start honing your economic survival skills.

Living Leaner

WHEN YOUR INCOME GOES INTO FREEFALL AND YOU'RE DESPERATELY scrambling to find work, the art of living frugally won't be an option—it'll be a strict necessity. Why wait until the axe falls? If you can start getting your financial house in order and saving some money, it will be that much easier to transition to a reduced standard of living should you get the sack. Even better, you'll be giving yourself a valuable financial crutch to lean on while you ponder your next move. It won't be easy. Old habits are often hard to break.

Most of us keep a close eye on our earnings, down to the last decimal point. However, when it comes to tracking where our money goes between paychecks, things start to get fuzzy. Unless you have a workable system in place to manage your money, it's going to be that much harder to cut back and save. Even if you've successfully devised a budget, you can expect a daily struggle to rein in your spending. Like a pack-a-day smoker who swears off his or her habit, backsliding will remain a constant threat. The mind is capable of all sorts of clever rationalizations, and it's easy to convince ourselves that a few small purchases won't make a difference. If you start to lose focus, try to keep in mind the gravity of your situation: You may not have a job in the future.

The best way to get started on your budget is to get a clear idea of your monthly expenses. The key is categorizing each expense—i.e., "Food," "Rent," "Gas," "Utilities," "Entertainment," etc. Using either a spiral notebook or a computer spreadsheet, document and categorize every single transaction over a thirty-day period. Once the month is over, you should have a pretty good idea of both your spending habits and your estimated expenses for each category. You will likely be amazed at how much of your money goes toward non-essential things. Now take your estimated monthly income and subtract what you consider absolute necessities like rent, car and mortgage payments, utilities and other essentials from this amount.

If you don't have any disposable income left over once you've allocated money for necessities, you're simply living beyond your means, and this will have to stop. Consider moving into a cheaper place, trading in your vehicle for something more affordable, and other measures that will significantly reduce your overhead. If you do have some money left over, focus on saving as much as possible. Even if you're coming out ahead each month after paying your bills, closely examine how much you spend for each category and try to find ways to lower these amounts. Set strict limits in your budget for non-essentials. The more you cut back, the more you will save.

You might encounter difficulties at first, but always remember that the process is ongoing. Each month you can make adjustments and try new approaches. If you have a bad month, just redouble your efforts in the future. Above all else, stay committed. If you're not sure how to get started, we've included a few helpful suggestions below:

Avoid Debt: This is a major pitfall. Limit the number of credit cards you own and try to reduce or pay off all your debts. If you have a crippling home mortgage or car loan that is eating away at your cash flow, consider walking away from these debts and shifting to a more modest existence. Bankruptcy will be discussed in greater detail later on, but if you find yourself unable to crawl out from under your unpaid bills, this might be your only realistic option.

Remember the Small Things: Sometimes it's not always the outsized purchases that eat away at our bank accounts: It's the seemingly inconsequential things we buy that accumulate over time. Take a good, long look at your typical weekend or workday and think about what you can do to reduce spending. Have you considered packing a lunch to work in lieu of eating out every day? How about brewing your own coffee instead of buying your daily Starbucks blend? These are the sorts of minor changes that will start saving you money in the long run.

Put It "On Hold": Many frugally-minded consumers set up a "thirty-day-hold" list of non-essential purchases that they might be planning. When you run across something that seems impossible to resist, enter the item in a computer document or notebook along with the date. Don't make the purchase until a full thirty days have elapsed. By then, it's likely you won't quite have the same "buy-or-die" exuberance, and you won't even need to make the purchase. Sometimes there's a very fine line between what we think we need and what we simply want. This is a good way to make that distinction clear.

Use the Library: For many frugal living enthusiasts, the library is something akin to a second home. There are books, DVDs and videos galore to borrow, any number of periodicals available to read, and the occasional lecture—and it's all perfectly free. This is a great way to scale back your entertainment expenses.

Deal in Cash: We live in the age of plastic commerce—and maybe that's the problem. When a large purchase is simply a few numbers on a credit card receipt, we often lose our sense of perspective. Try dealing strictly in cash for a while. When you have to open your wallet and pass a stack of bills across the counter, it can often bring home that you're spending far too much. Moreover, the necessity and added complication of repeatedly going to the ATM might keep your impulse buying in check, and you won't be tempted to add to your credit card balance. At the very least, use your debit card in lieu of a credit card; that way you can only spend what's available in your checking account, and you won't take on any new debt, but you'll still have the convenience of using a credit card.

Eliminate Cable: Most of us view our monthly cable bill as a strict necessity. It's not. Many of the cable shows we enjoy are increasingly becoming available to watch online. So why not eliminate a major monthly expense?

Buy in Bulk: Make a list of all the staple items you buy on a regular basis, i.e., toothpaste, soap, light bulbs, etc. Start stockpiling these products by purchasing at bulk discount outlets like Costco, or pay close attention to supermarkets in your area that might be offering discounts to consumers who buy in large quantities. Not only will you save on grocery costs, you'll find yourself making fewer trips to the grocery store, which will reduce your monthly fuel costs.

Make a List and Stick to It: When you go to the grocery store, limit your purchases to what's on your list. Don't wander through the aisles and toss things into your shopping cart that look tasty. This is one of the easiest ways to overspend on groceries.

Take in a Roommate: Sure, you might lose some privacy, but if you're renting a home or large apartment and have the extra space, cutting your rent in half is a good enough incentive to take in a boarder. You might know a friend or relative who is looking for a place. If you can work out an arrangement to share expenses, you'll save even more money. Paying half your normal rent will also help ease the pressure if you're laid off.

Slow Food: Most of us spend far too much money ordering takeout, buying fast food, dining in restaurants or relying on pricey microwavable dishes in lieu of preparing our own meals. Maybe it's time to reclaim the lost art of the home-cooked meal. Start buying fresh produce (or growing your own!) and learn to cook your meals from scratch. You'll save money, it's healthier and more nutritious and, chances are, you'll find that a home-cooked dinner prepared with fresh ingredients is often far superior to most restaurant and takeout fare.

Use Alternative Transportation: Whether it's walking, skateboarding, riding a bike, taking the bus or subway, or carpooling with a friend or neighbor, the less frequently you use your car to get around, the more money you can save on fuel costs and the less wear you'll put on your vehicle. It's also good for the environment and, best of all, your lifestyle won't be shackled to the price of oil.

Set Up an Emergency Fund: If you get laid off, you'll be scrambling to find work, and running out of money will only add to your sense of desperation. If you've started saving money, put some aside in an emergency fund. You want to be able to survive for at least a couple months without a steady income. Never draw from this account unless it's an absolute emergency. The more you've put aside, the more options you will have when you're looking for work.

Your Body

LET'S SUPPOSE YOU'VE METICULOUSLY PLANNED FOR THE WORST. You've streamlined your spending, kept to a tight budget and socked away every penny. Finally, the dreaded day arrives. One Friday afternoon, you're called into your supervisor's office and your mounting fears are confirmed: you've been laid off. Fortunately, you've at least made some contingency plans and you've become more economically resilient. Then the unexpected happens. The following day, while moving some furniture in your apartment, you violently throw out your back. Even the smallest movements leave you screaming in agony, and a visit to the doctor indicates that you'll be on your back for at least a couple weeks and it may take months of physical therapy before you'll be back to normal. Your job search will need to be postponed indefinitely.

Consider this scenario if you don't believe that your health and fitness are important to your economic survival. If there is widespread joblessness, many of us may lose our employer-sponsored health care benefits. Should you need medical attention, you may be forced to rely on county-run medical clinics that could be overrun by the sudden onrush of newly uninsured patients. Your level of fitness can also affect your future income prospects. If you look infirm when you're going to job interviews, employers might be less willing to hire you for fear you'll constantly be out sick. There is also the possibility that the only employment you'll be able to find could involve a certain amount of physical labor.

A regular exercise regimen is much like an insurance policy—every hour you spend building muscle and conditioning your body will make you that much more resistant to injury or illness. Developing a well-toned physique supercharges your immune system, protects against heart disease, increases bone density and has even been known to counteract depression. If you have health insurance, consider going in for a physical and discussing your future health prospects with a physician.

Start paying closer attention to your diet. Drink plenty of water. Try to eat fish at least a couple times a week. Sardines, salmon, herring and mackerel contain Omega-3 fatty acids that will enhance your immune system. Load up on fresh fruits and vegetables, particularly strawberry, cantaloupe, blueberries and broccoli, as they are rich in antioxidants and can help to combat a number of seasonal illnesses.

Motivation is often the most difficult hurdle we face when it comes to maintaining a well-rounded fitness regimen. Exercise takes discipline, and it's often demanding, but you'll be amazed at how quickly the human body will adapt to a few regular workouts. However, always remember to stretch and warm up your muscles before engaging in any sort of physical activity, as this will help you avoid both injury and possible soreness.

If you can't afford membership to a gym, you can work out at home. Bodyweight exercises are highly recommended. They don't take up a lot of space and can be performed just about anywhere. Start out slowly, doing sets of crunches, squats, push-ups, leg lifts and other simple exercises, and slowly add more repetitions over time. If you don't have access to weights, you can improvise by placing a few heavy objects in a suitcase or backpack, or filling up a couple of buckets of water. You can do curls, rows and a number of other lift variations. Be sure to balance your muscle-toning exercises with some form of cardio workout, which will strengthen your lungs and heart, and give you added energy. When you can, take a brisk walk, go running or use an exercise bike or treadmill.

Repetitive exercises aren't for everyone. If you need a bit more stimulation, take up a sport or activity that builds muscle, flexibility and endurance, like bicycling, hiking, the martial arts, running, boxing or yoga. While your time may be limited, if you set aside a half hour for exercise three to five times a week, you'll start seeing results. If you're unsure how to begin, web pages like exercisegoals.com and exrx.net can provide you some guidance.

Your Mind

WHILE YOU BUILD UP YOUR BODY, YOU MUST ALSO BUILD UP YOUR mind. Losing a job is ranked as one of the top ten most traumatic events you will face in your lifetime. Mounting fears over possibly losing your home, savings and way of life will only increase the psychological burden. Obviously there's a high probability that many of us will experience a certain amount of situational depression. However, by preparing for this eventuality now, you can cushion the blow and deploy some effective coping mechanisms to see you through the rough stretches.

It's often difficult to maintain a rosy outlook when facing unemployment and other difficulties. Yet you must learn to recognize the symptoms of depression and ensure that you can channel these periodic bouts of gloom into some form of meaningful endeavor. Your future economic survival will require razor-sharp critical thinking skills—and depression is known to cloud judgment, upset concentration, kill ambition and create an overall sense of apathy.

Plan ahead of time and prepare a list of possible measures you can deploy if your spirits start to sag. Your primary goal is to take your mind off your worries and maintain your mental balance. The important thing is to have a concrete course of action. Let's take a look at some creative ways you can avoid falling prey to depression:

Witness to History: We are entering a unique historical period, and observing the financial crisis as a spectator might give you a much-needed sense of perspective. Consider keeping a daily journal or blog, and recording your thoughts and feelings about how the country is changing and what the future might hold. Use the narrative approach as an outlet to give vent to your thoughts and feelings about the country's ordeal and/or your personal situation. Today we greatly value the published memoirs, letters and journals of people who lived through the Great Depression, and perhaps your efforts will one day be similarly treasured. Such a project may do more than just give your life a sense of meaning—if you choose to record your thoughts online or in a blog, you may find that you'll be helping some of your readers who are facing similar challenges.

Volunteer: If you're out of work and have a couple free hours each day, donating your time to a worthwhile charity is a good way to stay active and avoid hanging around the house brooding about your current difficulties. If you choose to work at a soup kitchen or homeless shelter, you may find that your current troubles won't seem quite so bad when compared to people who are destitute, and it will feel good helping others. If you have an activist streak, you might find it rewarding to work with a political organization, which might give you a greater sense of purpose. Each of us has skills and personal qualities that can help others in need. Everything from designing a web page for free to editing a neighbor's résumé will give your confidence a much-needed boost, and may lead to employment opportunities you may have never considered.

Learn New Skills: Why not use your downtime to embark on a course of self-growth? Learning a foreign language, mastering a difficult software program you never had the time to figure out, or simply becoming more self-sufficient by learning to perform basic household repairs are just a few ways you can keep busy and use your extra time to add to your current store of knowledge and increase your overall confidence.

Seek Support: Don't stand on false pride. Seeking outside support from friends and relatives is often a decisive factor in how we overcome life's challenges. There's a good chance that other people share your fears, and are dealing with some of the same issues. Try to maintain an active social life, and take the time to talk with those close to you about your worries or concerns. Sometimes the best advice comes from those who have a different perspective, or can look objectively at your situation.

Back to Nature: Sometimes a walk in the park, a day hike, or a weekend camping trip is a good way to escape the stresses of modern life and give yourself a break. Even better, communing with nature doesn't cost a dime, and it often shows us how the simpler, non-material things can often matter most.

Stay Active: As we've mentioned, a regular exercise regimen goes a long way toward keeping depression at bay. When you can overcome physical challenges, the mental obstacles never seem quite as difficult. And for a quick mental pick-me-up, nothing can beat the warm glow of a runner's high after an evening jog, or the sense of accomplishment you feel after you've met a challenging fitness goal. Deep breathing exercises and yoga have also proven to be excellent for reducing stress.

These are just a few general suggestions. Each of us will likely fine-tune our coping skills and find out what works best. However, if you are particularly prone to depression, consulting with a mental health professional for additional guidance might be advisable. However, you may want to be wary of the therapeutic establishment's over-reliance on antidepressants. Many of the same drugs known to counteract depression can often trigger suicidal thoughts, weight gain and a host of other negative side effects. Moreover, this may not be the best time to be walking around in a chemically-induced state of serene happiness.

No one likes being lectured about the benefits of healthy living, and it's unlikely you purchased this book for holistic lifestyle tips. Yet it's worth emphasizing that your mind and body are your two most valuable assets. You will need to be confident, clear-headed and in optimal health to meet the challenges of Depression 2.0.

Food Storage

TAKE A GOOD LOOK INSIDE YOUR REFRIGERATOR AND CUPBOARDS. Would you have enough food to survive if you ran out of money? What if a natural disaster left you temporarily stranded inside your home or apartment without food? Preparedness isn't just for survivalists anymore. If you're interested in covering all the bases, setting aside an emergency food cache is a worthwhile idea and a smart long-term investment.

The grocery inflation Americans experienced in late 2007 and early 2008 because of surging fuel prices and a weak dollar was an unsettling reminder how precarious our food situation can become. Recent government statistics indicate that there are already an estimated 28 million Americans relying on food stamps to survive.[1] Should we experience a major spike in oil prices or another wave of inflation, food prices could jump to unheard-of levels, and you'll be glad you stocked up.

Few of us are aware that the majority of American supermarkets rely on what is called the Just In Time (JIT) inventory system. Initiated by U.S. manufacturers during the 1970s, JIT reduces the labor and costs associated with maintaining a large inventory by placing a greater emphasis on the efficiency of suppliers and subcontractors. In other words, when your local food outlet runs out of pork ribs or strawberry ice cream, there aren't any additional boxes of these items on site; they are simply reordered and restocked. While the JIT system has helped reduce the operating costs of most retail outlets, it has made us all the more vulnerable to complications in the food supply chain, like energy shortages, labor unrest or natural disasters.

When the subject of emergency food comes to mind, most people immediately think of canned goods. While there's nothing wrong with supplementing your basic cache with a few tins of meat, fruit or vegetables from the supermarket to add variety, it is worth remembering that the shelf life of most canned food is only about twelve months. Moreover, the nutritional value of these items will tend to erode with the passage of time. If you do store some canned soups or vegetables, get into the habit of rotating your food stock so that you can replace the cans that are nearing expiration.

If you want to get the most bang for your buck, try buying food that is both freeze-dried and nitrogen-packed. This process locks in freshness and nutritional content, while ensuring that these foods can be stored at room temperature for years without spoiling. If you're unsure what to buy and don't want to go through the trouble of assembling a stockpile, you can go to vendors such as Emergency Essentials (beprepared.com), which offers supplies of various freeze-dried and dehydrated food items for emergency situations. Nitro-Pak (nitro-pak.com), another popular vendor, offers prepackaged food rations ranging from a few days to several months.

If you're finding it hard to figure out what you need, inquire with the Church of Jesus Christ of Latter-day Saints—the Mormons have long encouraged members to store a large food cache, and they offer a number of helpful ideas and guidelines to the public. The Church has set up an online food storage calculator at lds.about.com/library/bl/faq/blcalculator.htm that will give you a general idea of what to acquire to survive for an extended period of time. When making your calculations, keep in mind that the average adult male or female requires between 1600–1800 calories per day to maintain body weight. To ensure proper nutrition, it's a good idea to include an additional stockpile of vitamins and protein additives to supplement your diet.

Be sure to place your food in tightly sealed, oxygen-free, FDA-approved food-grade containers. Most wholesale food suppliers have food-grade plastic buckets and other containers that won't leak toxins into your food supply, and will keep insects and rodents from invading. Heat, moisture and sunlight can often degrade the quality of your food cache, so try to find a storage location that is cool, dry and dark. Never place your food containers on bare concrete. Sometimes concrete contains undetectable levels of moisture that can easily bleed into your food containers. Try to place your food on shelves or elevated platforms. Take the time to familiarize yourself with the food you plan on eating. If you can't stomach your emergency foods, you'll have trouble keeping your strength up should you need to rely on these items in an emergency situation.

Start Your Search

ANOTHER GOOD WAY TO PREPARE FOR THE POSSIBILITY OF UNEMPLOYment is to start laying the groundwork for your job search today. What are some ideas you might want to keep in mind? For one thing, when it comes to money, you may need to lower your expectations. Businesses will likely be struggling to survive, cutting back on staff and trying to limit expenses. Many of us may find ourselves forced to take a cut in pay and even benefits due to the impact of the current crisis.

The current job market is also going to be highly competitive. You'll really need to go the extra mile in terms of marketing yourself. In other words, avoid a one-size-fits-all approach with your résumé. You're going to need to tailor how you present yourself to meet the current needs of employers. When the economy isn't doing well, expectations often change. Try several variations of your basic résumé that focus on a couple different themes. A few points worth emphasizing are included below:

Multitasking: Are you the type of person that can take on several responsibilities at once, and learn new ones too? Staff cutbacks and company downsizing will likely leave employees in the unfortunate position of doing more for less. Human resource managers will be looking for flexible, creative individuals who possess a great deal of initiative. These are important qualities to stress on your résumé, as they will likely be in great demand for the foreseeable future.

Focus on the Bottom Line: While it's good to stress your experience, education and professional qualifications (and now more than ever), money will become the central issue to your prospective employers. When possible, emphasize how your previous job performance may have helped generate profits, increase efficiency or lowered overhead. It's not going to be easy selling yourself as either a moneymaking machine or a miserly cost-cutter, but these are the very qualities companies will be looking for.

Emphasize Commitment: There's nothing wrong with jumping from job to job. Some of us require a bit more stimulation than others, and believe that when you start dreading coming to work it's time to move on. If this is your workplace philosophy, you may need to repackage yourself as a Cold War-era "company man." Businesses are going to be strongly averse to hiring and training someone who plans on jumping ship at the first opportunity. While you can't exactly hide your employment history (and you wouldn't want to), at the very least point out that you are looking for a position with long-term potential, and possibly point out that you're willing to stay at least a year.

Once you've revised your résumé, there's nothing wrong with responding to a few of the job openings you might run across and going on a few interviews, just to sharpen your job-seeking skills and test the waters. The more you apply, the more you will have demystified the process, and you'll be less nervous when you encounter the real thing should you get laid off. Take the time to browse the want ads, and get a general idea of what types of companies are hiring and what job options are available. If the situation looks increasingly bleak, you might not even need to bother applying in your current field, and you may need to focus on securing a "survival" position to tide you over until the economy picks up.

Recession-Proof Jobs

A SERIOUS RECESSION IS ALSO A GOOD TIME TO CLOSELY EXAMINE your existing skills. Take a good long look at your employment history and make a list of your abilities and strengths. Is there anything that might translate into a viable career, or at the very least a source of income should you get laid off? Is there any sort of job training that might give you an edge in a recessionary climate? There are a few niche fields that may not be affected by the current crisis:

Protection: It's unfortunate, but rising crime often accompanies economic hard times, and there will likely be greater demand for security personnel. On the positive side, most guard positions require minimal training. However, if you want to carry a firearm and earn more money, you will need to be certified, fingerprinted and submit to a background check. However, don't worry about going into debt. Certification training runs somewhere between $75–$250, and you can complete the entire course in a day.

Caring for the Sick: Kiplinger's ranks positions in the health care field near the top of the magazine's recommended list of "recession-proof" jobs.[2] While this certainly isn't the best time to think about going to medical school, there's a big demand for people with expertise in medical billing and coding. Training can be obtained at your local community college at a relatively low price. There's also a growing demand for Licensed Vocational Nurses (LVNs) and Medical Assistants. These jobs don't require a nursing degree, but you will need to go through a certain amount of training to be licensed and certified. It's not as cheap as attending a community college, but it's better than going into debt for a four-year degree. If you like working with people and aren't squeamish about being around hospitals, if you focus on the medical field, you will always have a lifeline to cling to—there is never going to be a shortage of sick people.

Network and Communications Analyst: Even during the worst economic times, we're still going to be jabbering on our cell phones about the high cost of rice or uploading photos of our urban gardens to our photo blogs. So long as the communications infrastructure remains intact, there will be a heavy demand for knowledgeable technicians to keep the system humming. By the year 2012, the U.S. Bureau of Labor Statistics (BLS) predicts a growth in this particular field of over 50%.[3] While some positions may require a computer science degree, if you have the required hands-on experience and background in the field, you should be able to find a job. If you have an electronics bent and enjoy working with computers, you might consider obtaining a two-year degree at a community college or certified school. Your long-term career prospects will be greatly enhanced.

Military: If you don't have many marketable skills, can't afford job training and your background isn't exactly squeaky clean, a few years in uniform might be a good way to sit out the recession. While you will enjoy excellent benefits, free room and board, training and possibly a signing bonus, there's also a good chance you might find yourself dodging bullets in Iraq or Afghanistan. On the plus side, soldiers rarely get laid off, so it might be worth the gamble if you're looking for recession-proof employment.

Federal Government: For the most part, employees at the federal level aren't often held hostage to the ebb and flow of the free market. While there may be a smattering of layoffs when tax revenues drop, it's one of the safer job niches out there. The hiring process is excruciatingly long, and you'll probably have to fill out a mountain of paperwork, but the pay and benefits are usually competitive. Consider taking a look at USA Jobs (usajobs.gov), the federal government's official job listing site, and you might find a nice, safe niche to ride out the current crisis.

The positions listed above are just a sampling of what might be available, so don't feel discouraged if you consider the prospect of working behind a security desk or office cubicle a fate worse than death. In many respects, the next few years will require creative, versatile individuals who can't easily be categorized into a specific job niche, so take the time to explore what's out there.

Using the Web

DURING THE WORST DAYS OF THE GREAT DEPRESSION, WHEN AN estimated one in four Americans was out of work, desperate jobseekers would often travel hundreds of miles if there were even the most cursory rumor that a company was hiring. Fortunately, we live in the information age, and can now ascertain the economic conditions, job prospects and long-term potential of any region of the country through web pages, e-mail, news feeds, community blogs and bulletin boards. If you'd like to use the web for your job search, there are numerous pages dedicated to connecting applicants with possible employers. For example, you can post your résumé on job boards in your community on sites like Monster.com and CareerBuilder.com, or you can also set up an account with sites like Jobster.com and Yahoo's Hot Jobs site (hotjobs.yahoo.com). These sites provide search engines that enable you to browse through thousands of posted job listings.

Perhaps the most interesting innovation for the web-based job seeker is the growth of social networking sites which offer an effective medium to communicate with fellow professionals in your field, network with current and former colleagues, and interact with possible employers. Moreover, corporate recruiters and headhunters are also turning to social networking programs when looking to fill positions. The Web 2.0 phenomenon, which includes everything from the quirky but wildly popular Facebook.com to the more corporate-friendly LinkedIn.com, offers an effective way to do some pre-emptive outreach if you fear that your job is reaching the end of the line. If you plan on utilizing a social networking page to further your job search, there are a few ideas worth keeping in mind:

Put Your Best Foot Forward: Always remember, sometimes it's the smallest things that count the most. If your social networking page is poorly designed, riddled with typos or formatting errors, or simply lacks any sort of organization, potential contacts may conclude that you're someone who does things haphazardly. Moreover, people are more likely to return to a site that is easy to use, eye-catching and interesting to read. Express yourself in a clear, unpretentious manner and try to make sure your individual slice of the web is user-friendly, well designed and visually engaging. As in life, first impressions often count the most.

Assemble Your Working Network: Make sure you're connected to prior employers, co-workers and associates who can vouch for you should a would-be employer express interest in your résumé. It's a good idea to build a thriving network of fellow professionals, as this could be a great way to acquire leads about future or current employment opportunities.

Make It Personal: Posting your résumé, job history and qualifications is a good start, but employers will want to get a sense of who you are and what your personality is like. Be sure to highlight your interests, hobbies and other details about yourself that will give people a sense of who you are. Posting commentary about your current job, how you spent your weekend, problems you may have solved, the economy, or even recounting a humorous experience are the types of things that might make an impact on a future employer browsing your page.

Benefits

IF YOU PLAN ON COVERING ALL THE BASES PRIOR TO POSSIBLY LOSING your job, be sure to explore how your state disburses unemployment benefits. So long as you've been laid off or fired, you have the option of filing for unemployment in all fifty states. If you qualify, you will receive a percentage of your usual pay based on your average quarterly earnings to cover living expenses for up to twenty-six weeks (sometimes this period is extended to fifty-two) while you look for a new job. Filing for unemployment is a good idea if you want to avoid drawing down your savings while you're searching for work.

It usually takes a couple of weeks to process each claim, and for ease of access, most states provide online filing, or you can initiate your claim over the telephone through an Interactive Voice Response (IVR) system. Be sure to gather all the information that will be required, like your Social Security and driver's license numbers, your income information, recent work history and your employer's name, address and telephone number. The U.S. Department of Labor maintains an online directory of state unemployment providers at this address: workforcesecurity.doleta.gov/unemploy/agencies.asp. All you need to do is look up your state unemployment agency, and you can research how to go about filing.

To claim your unemployment compensation, you will be asked to affirm that you are "able and available to work" and that you are "actively seeking work." Once your eligibility has been confirmed, you will be notified by your state's unemployment agency what your benefit amount will be. To continue receiving benefits, you will be recertified every one to two weeks (depending on your state), which you can either do online or through your IVR system. You will be required to report any money you have earned through part-time or temporary work, and possibly asked to provide proof of your job search like the names of employers you may have contacted. Since 1987, the federal government has determined that unemployment compensation is a form of taxable income.

Coping with unemployment won't be easy, especially at a time of great economic uncertainty. While it is hoped that you will keep your current job, during turbulent times nothing is ever certain. Take the time to plan for every contingency. At the very least, you'll be that much more resilient and able to bounce back should you find yourself a casualty of the current economic crisis. If you can master living frugally and within your means, you may discover that life's enjoyments needn't come with a price tag. This realization may go a long way toward ensuring your future happiness, regardless of your employment status. •

Notes

1   Carney, Mike. "Experts Predict Record Number of Food Stamps as Economy Slumps," *USA Today*, March 31, 2008.

2   Burt, Erin. "Recession-Proof Careers," *Kiplinger's*, April 3, 2008.

3   "Fastest Growing Occupations Through 2012," Bureau of Labor Statistics (BLS), February 12, 2004.

CHAPTER 3

DOWN BUT NOT OUT
ECONOMICS FOR LEANER TIMES

Down but Not Out:
Economics for Leaner Times

YOUR WORST FEARS HAVE MATERIALIZED. YOU'VE LOST YOUR JOB and are barely scraping by. As the crisis mounts, your life may begin to seem unmanageable. At this point, you may find yourself at something of a crossroads. You can either watch your expenses pile up and let your anxieties mount—or take immediate action. It won't be easy. When you've grown used to collecting a regular paycheck, the ability to eke out a living and survive on less can prove to be a hard-won skill. You will need to marshal your creative powers and develop a well-trained eye for spotting untapped economic opportunities and novel ways of saving money.

Economic survival is primarily a matter of trial and error. Unless you're a financial genius, there's a pretty good chance you won't succeed with every moneymaking scheme or cost-cutting effort. While you may suffer frustrations and disappointments, always remember that every setback will only add to your storehouse of knowledge and increase your chances of success in the future. If you can drastically reduce your overhead and generate some additional money, you will be that much more in control of your destiny.

Saving Energy

IN A WORST-CASE SCENARIO, YOU MIGHT BE FORCED TO GO WITHOUT a job for an extended period of time. Once your unemployment runs out, your only recourse will be spending down your savings. When you don't have any income coming in and your bills are piling up, time becomes your fiercest enemy. Each passing month will bring you that much closer to destitution. Your frantic job search will be overshadowed by a palpable sense of desperation. Every job interview will leave you filled with anxiety. Don't let it get to this point—start chipping away at your monthly expenses.

DOUGLAS RUSHKOFF ON FINANCIAL METRICS AND THE ECONOMIC CRISIS

Douglas Rushkoff is the author, most recently, of *Life Inc.: How the World Became a Corporation and How to Take it Back* (Random House, 2009).

Q: *What's your perspective on Barack Obama and the economy?*

DR: Obama means the best, but we have to remember that he is working within a system; his perspective is presupposed by an economic model. And that model is biased toward those who have the means to accumulate capital, and against those who create real value. Obama said as much in his inaugural speech, when he spoke about finding ways to promote the interests of people who actually "do stuff."

Most of America's Founding Fathers foresaw this scenario. They had direct experience of the British East India Trading Company, a monopoly chartered by the crown. The monarchy wrote laws prohibiting colonists from generating value from the cotton they grew. They weren't allowed to fabricate clothes, for example. They had to sell cotton to the Company, at fixed prices, and buy back clothes from England.

The contemporary corporate economy works the same way—extracting value from the periphery to support debt payments to central banks. We have two separate economies going on—a speculative economy, which is the Wall Street economy, and the real economy, which is Main Street.

Most people are judging Obama's success through the metrics of Wall Street. Obama made a speech today and the Dow Jones average went down. Now, is that a good thing or a bad thing? It depends on your perspective. From my perspective, the stock market has already been exposed as a sham—a drag

For the most part, our biggest expenditures tend to revolve around fuel, food and shelter. These are the big-ticket items that can drain your savings in just a few short months should your income dry up. Let's begin with your monthly utility bills. While your monthly power bill might seem insignificant compared to some of your more pressing financial burdens, when you don't have a lot of money to spare, shaving a few dollars from your power bills can make a difference. Most of us passed through our formative years at a time when cheap fuel was the norm and profligate power use was considered an American birthright. However, if saving money is a priority, you will need to reorient your thinking. If you follow some of the suggestions below you should see a reduction in your monthly utility bills.

• Make sure you use compact fluorescent light bulbs (CFLs) for all your existing light fixtures. CFLs use less than 25% of the electricity required by traditional bulbs, and last up to ten times longer.

• If you have a washing machine in your home or apartment, wash your clothes in cold water whenever possible. Water heating accounts for a significant amount of the energy used to operate a washing machine. Forgoing the dryer and setting up clotheslines to air-dry your laundry is another great way to cut back your energy use.

• Consider switching to a laptop for your primary computing needs. Desktop models use far more energy.

• During summer months, avoid using the air conditioner when possible, limiting it to only brief, intermittent periods. Keep cooler by using fans (which are more energy-efficient) and closing doors and windows.

• Limit the water heating costs in your energy bill by installing low-flow heads in your showers and aerated faucets in your sinks, which greatly reduce the amount of water you use and will subsequently lower water heating costs. Check with your city's water department, as these plumbing fixtures are often provided to consumers at a discount or free of charge.

• Make it a habit to power down all computers, DVD players, gaming systems and other electronic equipment when not in use. If you don't plan on using your computer monitor for twenty minutes or more, turn it off. If you won't be using your computer for at least two hours, shut it down or use power management features like sleep mode.

on the real economy. If it goes up after Obama speaks, it means then that people's faith in the phantom speculative economy has increased and thus their faith in the real economy has decreased. If the market goes down after Obama speaks, then might that mean that people realize the pyramid shell game of a stock exchange is no longer the place to be invested in, and that it is much more important to be invested in real things or to be on the side of people who are creating value rather than that of people who are extracting it?

Q: *Do you believe a Wall Street crash could be beneficial to the real economy?*

DR: I think the crash of the speculative economy is very painful for the real economy because jobs are lost and we're living on a landscape where it's very hard to recuperate. We've grown so dependent on our corporations for money and for employment that it's very hard to just create new employment in a non-corporate way. But it is entirely within our ability. We just forgot.

Q: *What is the function of interest rates in a speculative economy?*

DR: Interest rates are the way that most of the money is made in our economy. Money is created at an interest rate; it's lent into existence, and there's a ladder of institutions that lend down to each other until it gets to the business or person that is supposed to be the end user of that money. But money becomes too top-heavy when there are too many institutions to support with every dollar that's borrowed. And eventually the system stops working. So then the central bank tries to lower the interest rates so that people can still borrow it.

I think the current problem is not that there aren't enough people offering credit, but there's not the demand for the product that the banks are creating. They try to generate demand for currency by giving out really cheap loans on houses. That really was not about real estate at all. The myth of an "ownership society" was developed in order to generate more business for bankers—more excuses to borrow money in order to "own." It's not a secret cabal of conspiring bankers. But the banking industry has become a purely extractive force, and it's healthier to watch that crash now of its own accord than to have the big bloody revolution that would happen if we don't. I'd much rather see the global

- Use caulking or weather-stripping on windows to seal off air leaks. Your home will be cooler in summer and warmer in winter, and you will reduce your A/C and heating costs.

- Investigate power-saving technology such as the PowerwoRx e3, a device that can be installed in your circuit breaker box that makes all the appliances and electronic devices in your home operate more efficiently and require significantly less power. For more information see SystemsToPurify.com.

- In cold weather regions, be sure to regularly dust and vacuum heating vents and radiators, as residual buildup makes it more difficult to adequately heat a room. Try placing blankets over doors and windows during the colder time of the year to lock in heat and limit cold. In a chilly bedroom, try using an electric blanket for a few minutes to warm the bed as opposed to cranking up the thermostat (use safely, as electric blankets can be fire hazards).

- Send e-mails or write letters instead of making expensive long-distance phone calls. You may even consider giving up your landline and relying entirely on your cell phone.

Transportation on the Cheap

IT'S DIFFICULT TO MAINTAIN A BUDGET WHEN GAS PRICES HAVE become increasingly volatile. When prices suddenly skyrocket, your entire monthly budget can be thrown into disarray. While your car may be a vital necessity, that doesn't mean that you shouldn't investigate cheaper alternatives like walking, riding a bike, ride sharing or public transportation. This is especially true if you reside in a pedestrian-friendly urban locale. Try going to WalkScore.com and see how your community measures up in terms of pedestrian access. Walking is more than just healthy, it's a great way to get to know your surrounding community, and you'll save a lot of money on gas.

Many cost-conscious consumers are opting out of car ownership altogether and signing on for car-sharing programs like Zipcar (zipcar.com). Users register with Zipcar for a $50 annual fee, and are issued a "Zipcard." When you need to drive somewhere, you simply make a reservation and then go to a Zipcar location. Swiping your card will unlock the vehicle of your choice, and the cost for use is $10/hour or approximately $75 for a full day. There are no economy level the playing field all by itself than to have our artificially wealthy nation stampeded by those whom we exploit.

Q: *Americans are now reliant on foreign manufacturers. Is there any way this trend can be reversed?*

DR: I think we have to decide what it is that we think we can do well. We can look at the law of comparative advantage, the basic premise of which is that at full employment if you do the thing that you do best and let others do what they do best, everyone's going to end up doing well. At less than full employment, the law of comparative advantage no longer functions. So we can't just say, "Oh, if we're good at microchips we'll do that, and let China do car manufacturing." That's only beneficial to everybody if everybody's fully employed.

And we've reached the point of diminishing returns in terms of industrial age, mass-produced goods. We've found out that the only way to increase profits in a mass production scheme is either to make production cheaper or get more people to buy more stuff in less time. We've reached the limits of both. We have outsourced production, used poisonous materials, exploited populations and polluted vast territory. We've also reached our limits of consumption. People just can't consume anymore, they don't want to. They no longer find the sense of satisfaction in it—all our possessions separate us from each other rather than bringing us together.

By leaving the growth requirement of the speculative economy behind, we have an opportunity to make better stuff and more sustainable stuff, and actually look at ways to work less hours. It's not a fantasy at all—just look at the many local and sustainable businesses in America today. There are enough around. Places where they design and manage and manufacture their stuff and even source the material in one area and either distribute really widely or distribute to a certain region.

If you're no longer indebted to the bank or to an interest-driven economy, then you're much freer to create a sustainable business model. So then it's not a matter of saving industry as we know it, but rebuilding a scaled set of businesses tied to the real world and the communities in which they are operating. That's not a pipe dream, that's really possible.

hidden fees or charges. Many consumers have found that they save a great deal of money relying on these kinds of car-sharing programs, and don't miss the expense and hassle of owning a car. If you're interested, CarSharing.net can direct you to programs in your community.

If you're spending too much on gas, there are also some proactive steps you can take to limit your monthly fuel expenses:

Lighten Your Load: Unless you're living in your car, avoid overloading your vehicle. The more excess weight you add to your car, the more gas you will burn.

Keep it Humming: Make sure that you take your car in for regular tune-ups, maintenance and oil changes. When the engine is functioning smoothly, it will require less gas.

Check Your Tires: When your tires aren't inflated properly, you'll be burning more fuel, and you can quickly wear out the treads.

Take it Easy: Stay within the speed limit. Driving at lower speeds improves your fuel economy. Fast starts and engine revving also waste precious gas.

Use Cash: Most service stations charge extra fees to consumers who use credit cards to purchase gas. Pay in cash and you'll save a bit of money.

Get Organized: Try to run all of your errands in one day, as opposed to making several small trips over the course of the week. Time your trips so that you can go when traffic is lightest, and you won't waste as much gas. If you need to stop at several places in the same vicinity, park your car in a central location and walk to your destinations.

Shelter

WHEN YOU'RE SHELLING OUT $1,500 EACH MONTH FOR RENT, AND you're having trouble finding work, it won't take long before your savings will start to run out. Moreover, should you fall behind on your rent you may not have enough money on hand to cover relocating to a new place. If you've recently

DOUGLAS RUSHKOFF continued

Q: *Doesn't this concept reconstruct the entire idea of profit making?*

DR: Not reconstructing, but reviving. It goes back to the people who are the supposed heroes of the corporate libertarians. Adam Smith was looking for a scaled economy of small businesses and farmers, and people doing things. He thought local businesses would always do better and the people would always prefer to do business locally because they're going to be biased toward the places where they live. It's not really a step backwards, it's more a step *through*. We don't have to move back to the hunter-gatherer stage. Just a human one.

Q: *Cities aren't particularly sustainable. What practical advice do you have for urban dwellers?*

DR: You can do urban agriculture and rooftop gardens and reduce the stress load and energy costs. But you're limited. I would think that people in urban areas can certainly sign on for Community Sponsored Agriculture, subscribe to a farmer, go out every couple of months and actually help. There's enough to do in the urban terrain as well. It's not like cities need to go away. You can contribute to your public school rather than sending your kid to private school. Take the $20,000 worth of time that you would have spent [on a private school] and spend those hours making a public school better. That way you're actually reinvesting in a city.

Cities do accomplish certain things well. Unless we have a sudden population decline, we're going to need people who are willing to stack up on each other like that for the rewards of getting to see lots of people, getting better nightclubs, bigger bookstores or whatever you might get. That's the only way we're going to cope with overpopulation.

As we spend less money on insulating ourselves from the poor, and we have more money to reinvest in our infrastructure, we can start looking at things other than flushing massive amounts of human waste into toxic chemical sewage. We can look at ways for cities to consume a lot less stuff and produce a lot less shit. That's not rocket science either; it's really just a certain amount of retooling.

suffered a foreclosure, you may find yourself in a similar bind. If you're not having much luck finding work, it might be a good idea to downsize your current living situation and consider something more affordable. It won't be easy—due to the subprime fallout, more Americans will likely be moving into apartments, and this could drive up rent. Try some of the following strategies if you're worried that your monthly rent check is becoming too big of a burden:

Roommate: As mentioned in a previous chapter, there is no better way to reduce your expenses than taking in someone to share the rent. Make sure that your landlord is aware of your decision, and try to find someone you know. If not, take out an advertisement in a local community paper or consider advertising on Craigslist.com. Find someone you can trust—if your roommate starts shirking on his or her portion of the rent, you won't just be back at square one, you will also have a dependent to support.

Rent a Room: The old American tradition of renting out a bedroom could soon become popular once more. Homeowners may be interested in earning extra income, and consumers who can't afford a regular apartment will begin looking for alternatives. Try asking around or advertising, and see if someone might be interested in letting you rent out a vacant room.

Move Back Home: Sometimes desperate times call for desperate measures. It might be a bit humbling, but there's nothing wrong with biding your time with family until the economic situation improves. Who knows? Your old room might be just like you left it.

Frugal Food Habits

WHEN YOUR BACK IS AGAINST THE WALL, CHANGING YOUR EATING habits won't be easy. Many of us tend to fall back on comfort foods when we're feeling stressed, and when you can't afford too many luxuries, loading up on a few choice cuts of meat or sugar-filled treats at the supermarket can be a constant temptation. However, if you're serious about lowering your monthly expenses you will need to adopt a more disciplined approach to how you buy food. You can still eat well—you will just need to go about things in a different way.

Q: *Is this what you mean when you describe the current financial crisis as a "unique opportunity"?*

DR: Yes. The other unique opportunity is the development of local and alternative currencies. In Washington and Oregon you've got the Fourth Corners exchange; there's also the LETS (Local Exchange Trading Systems) system, there's Time Dollars. There's lots of ways to earn money into existence rather than borrow it into existence. It could be as simple as starting a babysitting club where people earn babysitting hours for every hour they babysit. And maybe people will start being willing to accept babysitting hours as a unit of currency, as a standardized unit. You know, if you give me three babysitting hours, I'll give you this record, or I'll give you this book I wrote, or I'll give you this food I grew and then I'll spend the babysitting hours hiring another kid to babysit.

Q: *Do you mean a barter system as opposed to a Federal Reserve note system?*

DR: In a sense, but it doesn't have to be barter. Just real. Barter implies a two-way thing; that I get your thing and you get mine. Money—actual currency—allows for a third or fourth party to enter into the transaction. There's a restaurant in my town that needed money to expand and the banks weren't lending any more money. So the owner asked the community for money to expand, and the way we're paying him is by buying restaurant dollars. For every dollar we spend we get $1.20 worth of redemption at the restaurant. If you put in $500 you get $600 worth of food. That gives me a twenty percent return on my money—and it's money I'd spend anyway, because it's the only organic restaurant in town. Meanwhile, the restaurant owner gets the money cheaper than he'd get it from a bank. What's that? That's an alternative currency.

Look at the Eldercare dollar system in Japan where people needed their elderly to get taken care of during a serious recession when no one had money or jobs. They created an alternative currency system through which people could invest their time; you'd bathe someone's grandmother where you live, and you'd earn a certain number of credits for someone else to take care of your grandparents in a distant town. Each kind of task—like bathing, cooking meals or playing gin rummy—had a different, per-hour value attached to it. Hundreds of millions of dollars worth of health care was provided in this way in a country where no one had the money to buy it but everyone had time because they were all unemployed. And now that the economy has gotten better, the old people still

To understand why we always seem to go over budget when we shop for groceries, try to keep in mind that there's an underlying psychology to how food is displayed at the supermarket. For example, a tactic called "eye-level marketing" ensures that the most expensive products will always be most visible to consumers. Another common strategy involves placing staple items near the back part of the store so that you'll be tempted to toss various non-essential goods into your shopping cart while you make the lengthy trek to the meat or dairy section. If you've ever wondered why there's always a line at the various checkout counters, some store managers will limit the number of cashiers on duty so that people will spend more time inside the store.

These are just a few of the clever stratagems used by supermarkets to keep us buying what we don't need. However, it isn't all that hard to outwit these subtle behavioral cues. For one thing, never go to the supermarket when you're hungry. Your resistance will easily break down if you run across something that looks particularly mouth-watering. Wait until you've had a hearty meal, and then take care of business. However, before you even set foot inside the store, make sure that you have a comprehensive shopping list in hand and stick to it with an almost monk-like devotion. Don't allow yourself any exceptions. Plan ahead and even consider making out weekly or monthly menus so that you can handle all of your shopping needs in a single trip each month. The fewer times you have to go to the store, the less temptation.

Once you've got your shopping habits in check, let's take a look at some other ways you can pare down your food expenses:

Coupons: If you're really serious about staying within your budget, coupons will come in handy by reducing your monthly grocery bill. Most supermarkets post coupons on their web pages for easy access. However, don't fall into the trap of buying something just because you have a coupon. Limit your coupon shopping to items you purchase on a regular basis.

Carb-Loading: Atkins Diet aside, there's nothing wrong with a hearty meat-free dinner a couple times a week. If you can load up on pasta or a rice dish every other day, you won't need to buy as much meat, and you'll save money. At the very least, consider opting for inexpensive sources of protein like canned tuna, lentils, cheeses, peanut butter or beans.

Shop in Seasons: Familiarize yourself with what fruits and vegetables are in season each month, as that's when prices tend to drop.

DOUGLAS RUSHKOFF continued

prefer their health care to be given to them through the Eldercare system than through the professional retail system, because the care turned out to be better, higher quality and more human.

Q: *Do you envision similar alternatives to housing, i.e., eco-villages, co-housing, etc.?*

DR: People are going to come up with their own models. And there are a lot of alternatives in-between renting from an evil landlord and creating a commune. There are a lot of steps between those things. People are going to find the place that they're comfortable. The most significant thing that could take place is simply for people to realize that there's more than one model for life and commerce out there. As soon as we start to realize that there are things we need in this world other than money, we find out there's ways we can pay and participate in society other than with money—certainly other than the centralized bank paper we currently call money.

Q: *Do you believe people will start adopting these measures and moving away from the 7-Eleven consumer mindset?*

DR: People don't generally abandon consumer capitalism unless their feet are held to the fire. We have some very well constructed myths of wealth and currency. Sometimes the only way for those myths to get shattered is through shock and awe. The fact that America now has a crisis may be enough to jostle us loose from our death grip with bank-driven capitalism.

Q: *Have you seen anything recently that has changed your perspective of what's happening with the economic crisis?*

DR: It's bumming me out that the metrics people are using to gauge the economic crisis are actually the metrics that indicate how shackled we are to the failed model. Mortgage rates and stock averages are not true signs of prosperity. They are life signs of the dying capital infrastructure. But I'm encouraged by how innovative people are being and how they're not seeing every social and economic innovation as part of a weird, lefty communal paradigm. And when people actually do it, it seems entirely normal and real. •

For example, summer is the best time to buy cantaloupe, strawberries, watermelon, lettuce, tomato and green beans.

Go Local: Don't limit yourself to the supermarket. If there is a local farmer's market or farm in your area, you might be able to get some of your produce at a bargain. When farmers don't have to pay exorbitant shipping and transport costs, they'll often pass the savings on to consumers. You can also investigate Community Supported Agriculture (CSA) programs. These initiatives allow you to invest in local farms and receive fresh produce at an affordable cost.

Avoid the Corner Store: Buying grocery items at 7-Eleven or the nearby liquor store may be convenient, but the food and beverages are usually overpriced. Try to limit your shopping to a few different outlets where you won't be overcharged.

Freeze It: Don't let good food go bad by letting it sit in the refrigerator or on the kitchen counter. Freezing fruits, vegetables, cakes and other dishes is a great way to stretch your food budget, and you won't be needlessly tossing out food.

Watch for Bread Bargains: A lot of breads and rolls have to be taken off of the shelves by a certain date, and can be purchased at a reduced price. You can then store the breads in your refrigerator or freezer for increased longevity.

Dumpster Diving

ALTHOUGH STATISTICS VARY, BETWEEN ONE-FOURTH AND ONE-HALF of all edible food in the U.S. is tossed into the garbage each year by supermarkets, restaurants and consumers. Moreover, scads of valuable computer equipment, books and furniture are also needlessly thrown away. This is where you come in. If you'd like to lower your grocery bills, enjoy a diverse diet or are considering a small-scale retail business, dumpster diving is a great cost-free activity that is well worth exploring. Be warned: It's not for the fastidious or self-conscious. You're probably going to encounter some noxious odors, filthy and possibly rancid garbage and maybe even a few disdainful stares from random onlookers. Nevertheless, don't let these minor obstacles deter you.

Before you get started, be sure you have a pair of heavy gloves, some thick-soled boots, old work clothes, a flashlight, a thick rucksack for storing your finds and a stick for poking through the garbage. Some dumpsters may contain harmful industrial chemicals, so be sure to wear your gloves at all times. Avoid climbing into garbage bins—the heavy steel lid could come crashing down at any time, and you could be severely injured. Be sure to clean and disinfect anything you might bring home that has been inside a dumpster. Some experienced urban scavengers recommend bringing a friend along. You'll have the advantage of two sets of eyes, and one of you can serve as a lookout if you're operating in a more security-conscious area.

In most localities, dumpster diving is technically legal. However, some businesses, homeowners and landlords may try to discourage your efforts. Always try to be conciliatory and never make a mess, or your garbage site may be locked away or placed off-limits. Some municipalities have started outlawing garbage scavenging, so take the time to research what the laws are in your vicinity. If you want to deploy a bit of subterfuge to your efforts, consider wearing a pair of blue coveralls or a white butcher jacket, and people may mistake you for a city employee or a supermarket staffer.

If you're just getting started, pay close attention to your surrounding community. Are all trash bins locked or walled off? If that's the case, you'll need to focus more on residential garbage and target dumpsters in another area that's a bit more relaxed with trash disposal. So where do you begin? Let's examine a few choice locations:

Supermarkets: If food is your main priority, your typical supermarket or food mart should be your starting point. Supermarkets are constantly tossing perfectly good food. Whether it's slightly bruised (but perfectly edible) fruits and vegetables, TV dinners or frozen vegetables that may have a bit of freezer burn, or quality canned food that's been tossed to make room on the shelves, you'll generally run across more than a few items to stock your pantry. However, be sure to wash all fruits and vegetables you might pick up, and pay close attention to expiration dates on the packaging. Sometimes you might encounter broken glass if jars have been tossed, and a small minority of store owners have even taken to dumping bleach on discarded food, so be very wary if you detect any strong industrial smells. As long as you're discriminating, you should run across some great finds, but never take risks with food that may be questionable or outdated—as the old saying goes, "When in doubt, throw it out."

Bakeries: This is another frequent stopping point for enterprising garbage hounds. If you can find a dumpster outside a bakery that is easily accessible, you won't need to worry about bread for quite a while. The selling point for most bakeries is the fact that the cakes, doughnuts, breads and other products they offer are freshly made and still warm. Thus, at the end of each day, all sorts of baked goods get tossed, often wrapped in plastic or still in boxes. Even the stalest of breads can be put in the microwave or used for making croutons or French toast. If you can locate a good bakery with a wide-open dumpster it will be well worth your time.

Apartment Buildings: Apartment building dumpsters can often hold a veritable treasure trove of consumer swag. People are always moving out and needlessly tossing valuable items because they may be moving to a smaller place or want to simplify their packing. You might run across everything from a home computer to a working television set. A good rule of thumb is to check apartment dumpsters at the end of the month when people may be moving out.

These are just a few suggestions. Over time you will likely develop your own preferences as you start exploring different locations. Some people swear by Starbucks (if you don't mind a few coffee grounds in your pastries), while those who favor books and periodicals will target a Borders or Barnes and Noble. The dumpsters that adjoin college dorm rooms are often cited as a goldmine for food and valuables. Apparently if you show up on the last day before students have to move out of the dorms at the end of the school year, you can run across some amazing finds.

The important thing is to start viewing trash as a resource, as opposed to just waste. Depending on your aptitude and ability, dumpster diving can work on several different levels. If you're the mechanical type, you might run across a goldmine of electronics equipment and other valuables that can be repaired and resold at a profit. If you have a background in sales or marketing, you might spot things like clothing, books, dinnerware or furniture that you can peddle at a flea market or garage sale, or on eBay. If you'd simply like to lower your expenses, you'll run across food, clothing and other items that will help reduce your overhead.

However, it may take a while to develop your scavenging skills. If you'd like to exchange information and possibly glean some experience from seasoned veterans, there's a dumpster diving Meetup site online that will direct you to fellow enthusiasts in your area at dumpsterdiving.meetup.com. If you can find it, you won't go wrong with John Hoffman's informative and highly entertaining treatise on the subject, *The Art and Science of Dumpster Diving.*

Urban Gardening

IF ROOTING THROUGH GARBAGE SOUNDS UNAPPEALING TO YOU, LET'S focus on another way you can enhance your self-sufficiency and alleviate your food worries: setting up an urban garden. Growing your own food will lower your grocery bills. It's also healthy and beneficial for the environment, and there is something truly therapeutic about watching your well-tended garden grow and eating food that you've cultivated yourself. As an added plus, if you're enterprising, you can even sell some of your produce.

If you live in a cramped studio apartment or tiny suburban condominium, you may think you simply don't have the room for a garden. Fortunately, there are a number of home cultivation options that don't require all that much space. There are window box, container, hydroponic and even rooftop gardens. Some cities even have community gardening programs that allow you to utilize outdoor space to cultivate your own garden.

Your first step is finding an appropriate location, and this may be a challenge. If you plan on outdoor cultivation, keep in mind that you will need to ensure that your plants get several hours of direct sunlight per day, and you can't place your garden too far from your preferred water source. Some suggested locations include hanging potted plants from doorways or outdoor stairwells; setting up your garden on a fire escape, balcony or roof; using a window box; or even using some indoor space for a basic hydroponic garden. For most people in urban settings, container gardening may be the best option.

Not only do containers allow you to grow an eclectic assortment of different plants, the portability of the containers gives you the option of rotating plants into your home or apartment should excessive heat or rain threaten the health of some of your more delicate herbs or vegetables. It's also a great way to add some interesting color to the area around your apartment or home. You can also find a wide assortment of containers made from clay, terra cotta, wire, plastic and wood, to name just a few. If you're the creative type, you can even make your own.

Before you decide what to grow, take into account your space limitations. Some fruits and vegetables quickly outgrow containers and require additional space, while others will adjust to the limited space with some pruning. In terms of growing options, the sky's the limit. Using a good-sized container, you can grow beans, lettuce, tomatoes, broccoli, thyme, Rosemary, carrots, garlic, squash, potato, cherries, blueberries and dozens of other herbs, fruits and vegetables. For sheer versatility, containers offer some amazing gardening opportunities. If you'd like more information, UrbanGardeningHelp.com, ContainerGardeningTips.com and HomeGrownEvolution.com are highly recommended as online resources for the would-be urban gardener.

If you simply don't have the space, there are a selected number of plants that can be grown indoors—or you can cultivate your fruits and vegetables hydroponically. Hydroponics is not a new technique—the concept of cultivating plants in nutrient-rich water and fertilizer is hundreds of years old. In many respects, a hydroponic garden will be far less burdensome if you only have limited time to tend your garden. Because the plants are grown in a completely controlled environment, you won't need to worry as much about pests, weeds or plant disease. It is also believed that vegetables grown with hydroponics are tastier, provide a bigger yield and are more nutritious than traditionally cultivated vegetables. If you'd like to learn more, try visiting CropKing.com for information about workshops, vegetable cultivation and obtaining hydroponics equipment.

If you'd like to enjoy the traditional gardening experience, look no further than the American Community Gardening Association (ACGA). The organization maintains an online database of community-based gardens throughout the nation, and can help connect you with a local garden in your vicinity. The web page is acga.org. If you don't have a garden in your area, and you're not the joining type, the ACGA also offers assistance and advice for those interested in setting up a local gardening project. You have much to gain by meeting and networking with people in your area who are dedicated to self-sufficient living, and some of the more experienced members will be able to pass along their gardening knowledge to you. You will also have a group of associates who might be interested in trading or bartering fruits and vegetables during leaner times, so that you can add more variety to your diet.

If cultivating a garden sounds far too labor-intensive, foraging for wild fruits, herbs and edible plants is another useful skill to have when you're trying to get by on less. Cattails, dandelions, wild fruits and berries, and a number of other edible plants can often be found growing wild in urban settings. Take the time to familiarize yourself with the variety of nutritious plants and herbs that may be growing in your area, and be sure to monitor how each plant may change over the course of the year. For safety reasons, it's important that you eat only those plants that you can identify with absolute certainty. *Edible Wild Plants: A North American Field Guide* by Thomas Elias and Peter Dykeman is an excellent source of information for those interested in foraging for wild food.

It's a good idea to avoid any wild plants growing near homes or apartments, as they may have been sprayed with pesticides. You should also try to keep away from plants that sprout near possibly contaminated rivers and lakes, as well as roadside shrubs and weeds, which are often tainted by vehicle emissions. Avoid mushrooms as a rule of thumb, as the risk of accidental poisoning may outweigh any nutritional benefit they might have. For a basic primer on survival foraging, Wilderness-Survival.net is an excellent choice.

Sources of Income

WHEN YOU'RE OUT OF WORK AND COMPANIES AREN'T HIRING, GENERating income can be difficult. If your primary focus is finding any kind of survival job to tide you over, registering with a temporary agency might be a good strategy to at least get back to work. As companies scale back staff, there will still be a pressing need for additional workers to cover for people on vacation or to help complete labor-intensive projects. Some of the larger agencies, like Manpower (manpower.com) even offer benefits to employees. Of course temp agencies take a cut from any money you earn, but this might be a good way to get back to work and make connections with employers, and there is also the possibility that a temporary position could evolve into a permanent job.

Temp agencies are also a good way to add more flexibility to your work schedule. If you'd prefer to concentrate on your job search for part of the week, you can make arrangements with the agency to only be called for work assignments on specific days. If you're thinking about temping, it's probably a good idea to register with more than one agency. As unemployment rises, there will likely be stiff competition for what temporary positions are available. Check your telephone book to see what agencies serve your area. You will probably be asked to register in person, as they will want to give you a skills test and read through your résumé.

Starting a home-based business is another possibility. However, you're going to be in something of a bind. If you're short of money, whatever business you pursue is going to require very little operating and start-up capital. Moreover, it won't be easy marketing and selling a product or service in the middle of a serious recession.

On the positive side of things, it has never been easier or more inexpensive to set up a business. The flyers, advertising and brochures that once required paying a professional printer can now be created in a few short minutes on your home PC using a simple word processing program. You also have the advantage of using the internet to network, make contacts, and promote your business, through sites like LinkedIn, Facebook and MySpace.

If you've always dreamed of being your own boss and dropping out of the 9-to-5 rat race, the current economic situation might offer you both the opportunity and the time to develop a business. If you already have some marketable skills, one of the more common types of self-employment is simply subcontracting your abilities to outside employers. In recent years, freelance writing, web design, coding and administrative work have become growing sectors of the economy. More and more Americans are working from home doing freelance work, and businesses are finding it more cost-effective to subcontract with a freelancer than to contract with a larger firm or create a permanent staff position.

Successful freelancing requires energy and dedication. Some work assignments, especially if you're working under a deadline, may prove more exhausting than a regular full-time job, and working on weekends is not uncommon. Along with the tension-filled weeks when you're struggling with a deadline, there may be dry periods when you can't seem to land work. Living in the present won't be an option. Once you've completed a project, no matter how tired you might be, you will need to redouble your energies and start looking for new assignments. "The check is in the mail" will become a familiar refrain, as freelancers often aren't paid on time and sometimes will wait weeks or even months before payment is received.

However, you can set your own hours and be your own boss, and for many individuals that's of far greater importance. It's also a lot easier to get freelance work thanks to the internet. If you have a background in writing, editing, data entry, programming, web design or social networking technology, you might try registering with Elance.com, which allows you to place bids on short-term work projects. Guru.com is another popular site for freelancers looking for work, as is Craigslist.com.

Freelancing isn't for everyone, and you may be leaning toward something a bit more basic. Perhaps what you have in mind is something that will provide a slow but consistent revenue stream that can tide you over until you've found work, or possibly something that might work out as a second source of income even if you do find a full-time position. Try out some of the ideas listed below—they won't require a great deal of money to get started, and over time, they could start generating some cash:

Moving: The recent epidemic of foreclosures is forcing people to move out of homes and relocate in record numbers. If you own a truck or van, consider putting your vehicle to work and assisting people who may need a low-cost mover. You can also branch out into other fields, like hauling brush or garbage, or subcontracting as a courier or delivery truck driver.

Scrap Metal: If you have a truck or van and ample storage space, peddling scrap metal is the kind of business that can start bringing in money immediately. Start small with aluminum cans, and put your scavenging skills to work at dump sites, garbage bins and garage or yard sales, where you might run across electrical wiring, used car batteries and other articles that contain lead, brass, iron, steel, copper and other base metals. Let people in your neighborhood know that you're interested in old stoves, car batteries and metal fixtures and that you'll remove them free of charge. Advertising in your community newspaper or on Craigslist may also be a good idea.

Employment Consultant: When people are desperate to find work, they'll do anything that will give them an edge. If you have a writing background and good formatting skills, you might try setting up a service in your community to help individuals seeking work. You can design résumés and compose cover letters, and for an added fee even help prospective job seekers set up a Facebook or LinkedIn page to show to prospective employers.

Buyer/Seller: This may require a bit of capital up front, but buying low-cost items at garage and yard sales and reselling them on eBay may prove to be a profitable sideline if you have a good eye for value and can gauge public demand. People tend to look for bargains and buy things used when the economy isn't doing well. You might also consider selling other people's valuables on consignment for a cut of the profits.

Personal Organizer: If frugal living becomes a national trend, people may be willing to pay someone to help organize their clutter, assist with budgeting and streamline their lifestyle. If you're the type of person that thrives on challenge, are good with figures and have top-notch organizational skills, then this may be a profession to look in to—and one that may be in high demand in the years to come.

Desperate Measures

SOMETIMES YOU MAY NEED A QUICK CASH INFUSION, AND WAITING isn't an option. Maybe it's an overdue phone bill, some emergency groceries or an unpaid parking ticket. Should you find yourself in dire straits, try the suggestions listed below:

Donate Your Plasma: There are hundreds of collection centers throughout the U.S. that offer cash in exchange for plasma. However, you will need to be in good health, and you can't have any drugs in your system or compromising health conditions. If you pass through the initial health screening (which takes about two hours) and are declared fit to donate plasma, you will generally receive $20–35 in compensation each time you donate. If you're interested, check your telephone book for the nearest plasma collection center. Because the human body replenishes plasma faster than blood, you can donate up to twice a week. However, be sure to eat something at least two hours before you go, and drink plenty of water. If you're lucky enough to possess a rare or unique blood type, or your plasma contains specific antibodies that are in demand, you may even be designated a "special plasma seller" and you'll be placed in a higher compensation bracket.

Sell Your Hair: If you've often been complemented on your lustrous, shiny locks, you might consider selling your hair as an emergency measure. Manufacturers of wigs and hair extensions have spawned a small market in human hair. Your hair generally needs to be at least ten inches long, and as a "natural" shine is the industry standard, your hair cannot be chemically treated. It is also advised that you avoid shampooing every day, as this drains the hair of important oils. While you can fetch as much as a thousand dollars, the price depends on many variables like length, color, thickness and shine. It's not hard to peddle your hair; simply post a photo on HairTrader.com. It's a pretty good idea not to cut your hair off until you've closed the deal. Most hair buyers prefer that you have your hair cut off by a salon and wrapped into a braid.

Sperm Donation: If you're a male between the ages of 18–34, you might consider donating your sperm. Check your telephone book for sperm banks and fertility clinics. You'll be asked to come in and submit a sperm and blood sample. You'll also be asked to complete an exhaustive questionnaire detailing your health and genetic history. The latter may require some additional legwork on your part, as some sperm banks require data about your family history going back four generations. Others may also include a rigorous psychological examination. If you meet all the various requirements and your sperm is judged to be of good quality, you will be asked to enter into a contractual agreement to provide samples for a set period that is usually between six to twenty-four months. Compensation can range from under a hundred dollars per sample and upwards into the thousands.

Research Subject: Why not contribute to scientific progress and get paid at the same time? College students have been volunteering as research subjects for years. If you live near a large university, there are usually advertisements posted in campus newspapers and on bulletin boards requesting research subjects. You can also check online at GPGP.net, which maintains a national directory of ongoing research that requires participants for everything from sleep deprivation studies to consumer focus groups. As with any medical or psychological procedure, it's probably a good idea to go into it with your eyes wide open and make sure you are aware of any possible risks. If you have any doubts or misgivings, try another research study.

Pawn Your Valuables: Most pawnbrokers can smell desperation a mile away, but if you're really in dire need, pawning a few of your possessions might be your only option. Don't expect to get a lot of money—but on the plus side, the less money you get, the easier it will be to redeem your possessions.

When your finances are in a perilous state, life can be challenging. Hopefully some of the suggestions we've covered in this chapter will at the very least provide you with a basic game to fall back on should you counter any difficulties. Always remember that adversity can often prove to be a catalyst for growth. The economic coping skills you develop today will make you stronger and that much more resilient in the future. •

CHAPTER 4

WALKING AWAY
THINKING ABOUT
BANKRUPTCY

Walking Away: Thinking About Bankrutpcy

IN THE POPULAR MIND, THE PROSPECT OF GOING BELLY-UP AND SEEK-ing legal refuge from one's creditors is an unseemly business at best, and a form of ritual humiliation at worst. As an old saying goes, if capitalism were a religion, these solemn courtroom proceedings would be the closest equivalent to hell. Unfortunately, in recent years Americans have been going bankrupt in record numbers. For the better part of this decade, an average of 1.5 million consumers have declared bankruptcy each year.[1] To give this number some historical context, in the year 2003 alone more people filed for bankruptcy than throughout the entire 1960s.[2] And we haven't seen the worst of it.

Spiraling credit card debt, depleted savings and hefty mortgage payments have pushed many consumers to the brink of insolvency—and the nation's current economic troubles will only add to this powerful undertow. When your income dries up because you've been laid off, or you're forced to rely on credit cards to meet your expenses, going under isn't all that hard. Whatever your opinion of bankruptcy, if you're penniless and straining under a mountain of debt, it might prove to be one of the best decisions you can make. The process can prove difficult, but it can also provide you with a much-needed lifeline and a chance to resurrect your troubled balance sheet. Indeed, you may find that the social stigma that surrounds bankruptcy is far preferable to losing your home or spending every waking hour being hounded by aggressive bill collectors.

We've all made foolish financial decisions. The important thing is not to compound these errors by liquidating your retirement account or taking other desperate measures because false pride won't let you admit to yourself that you've lost control of your finances. So long as you still have assets worth protecting, bankruptcy is a way to move forward with at least some of your hard-won possessions intact. Sometimes life deals you a bad hand. In this instance, you've hit rock bottom in the middle of an epic financial crisis. Now isn't exactly the best time to start hoping for miracles. If your economic survival is at stake, it might be well worth your time to familiarize yourself with how the bankruptcy process works.

A Brief History

WHEN WE LOOK BACK THROUGH AMERICAN HISTORY, PERHAPS WE can consider ourselves fortunate that over the past century bankruptcy laws have undergone something of a radical transformation. Our colonial forefathers weren't quite so lucky. In early America, bankruptcy provisions were strongly influenced by British laws that viewed the inability to pay one's bills as a serious criminal offense punishable by death or imprisonment. Under the British model, only the creditor could institute a bankruptcy action, and punitive justice was meted out to the unlucky debtor.

Thus, in the colonies, when a settler went broke, he was often locked up until his debts were repaid or his property was sold to the satisfaction of his creditors. However, bankruptcy provisions often varied among the different colonies, and some parts of the country were more forgiving than others. While our antecedents may have been thrifty and hard-working, they weren't immune to economic hard times, and financial failure was not uncommon. Whether caused by poor crops, bad investments, fraud or just plain bad luck, it wasn't hard to lose everything. Historian Kenneth L. Kusmer observes that there are records dating back to the 1640s describing the presence of penniless "vagrant persons" wandering through Boston.[3] By the 1750s, reports of indigent beggars in large commercial cities like Philadelphia and Baltimore had become commonplace.

Following the Revolutionary War, the U.S. Constitution placed bankruptcy under federal jurisdiction, and President John Adams signed the first statute dealing with bankruptcy into law in 1800. The bill was enacted after a speculative property boom collapsed, resulting in huge unpaid debts. Viewed as a temporary measure, the legislation allowed lenders to institute bankruptcy proceedings against delinquent borrowers. Usually whatever assets the unlucky party had in his possession were split among the competing creditors. Although the law was later repealed in 1803, another financial collapse in 1837 led to the passage of a new bankruptcy law in 1841—which was also repealed a few years later.

It wasn't until 1898 that a permanent bankruptcy statute was enacted, and a more forgiving approach toward debtors began to take root. The Bankruptcy Act of 1898 was one of the first bankruptcy laws that addressed the needs of the insolvent. In accordance with the pioneering new legislation, debtors were allowed to retain some of their possessions, and the bankruptcy courts forgave some debts so that the borrower could make a fresh start without the added burden of repaying outstanding financial obligations.

After decades of legal experimentation, the modern form of bankruptcy we know today was codified into law in 1978 with the passage of the Bankruptcy Reform Act. The new law, like its predecessor, placed a greater emphasis on the debtor and included important provisions that would allow the consumer to restart his or her economic life. Keep this in mind when considering whether or not to file: today's bankruptcy laws are designed to help, not hinder, your future financial prospects—for the most part.

Filing for Chapter 7 (Liquidation) Bankruptcy

THE MOST COMMON FORM OF CONSUMER BANKRUPTCY IS A CHAPTER 7 or "liquidation" bankruptcy, and is considered the least burdensome form of legal relief from debt. Unfortunately, this doesn't mean it's going to be quick and easy. The process begins when you (or your attorney) submit a voluntary petition to the bankruptcy court that serves the area where you live. However, it's a bit more onerous than merely initialing a form. Your petition must include the following items:

- Schedule of your current assets and liabilities.
- Schedule of your current income and expenditures.
- Statement of financial affairs.
- Schedule of any existing contracts and leases.
- A copy of your most recent tax return and any previous returns that were filed during the bankruptcy period.
- A detailed list of all of your current creditors (including name, address and telephone), the amount owed to each and the nature of each outstanding amount.
- A statement of your estimated income and source(s) of income.
- An itemized list of your property.
- A detailed list of your necessary monthly expenses, i.e., food, clothing, utilities, rent or mortgage, taxes, etc.

If you are filing to seek legal relief from primarily consumer debts, you will need to submit the following additional materials to qualify for Chapter 7 protection:

- A certificate that you have undergone credit counseling and any debt repayment plans that you agreed to as part of your counseling.
- A statement of monthly net income.
- Evidence of any money earned (i.e., copies of paychecks) sixty days prior to filing and any documents showing any projected increase in either income or expenses after filing.
- If you have any money invested in any federal education or tuition accounts, you must provide the appropriate documentation.

The official bankruptcy forms can be purchased at most legal stationery stores or downloaded free of charge at uscourts.gov/bkforms/index.html. It's very important that you make sure all the information is accurate, as you can be penalized if there are any inaccuracies, or the bankruptcy court has reason to believe you have falsely represented your financial status (even if that was not your intent). Before you can officially file, you will be required to pay a $245 case filing fee, an additional $39 miscellaneous fee and a $19 trustee surcharge. However, if you are in dire poverty, the court may allow you to pay these amounts in installments or possibly waive the fees altogether.

Once the court receives your petition and your case is officially filed, something called an "automatic stay" goes into effect that protects you from the majority of your creditors. In essence, you are under the protection of the bankruptcy court. If you are facing lawsuits, possible eviction or foreclosure, garnishment of wages, or threats of repossession, the automatic stay extends a legal shield that temporarily blocks these efforts. Your creditors will be contacted and informed of your status, and this should provide some much-needed relief.

A short time after you've filed for bankruptcy, a hearing will be held and you will be placed under oath. A court-appointed trustee and possibly your creditors will be allowed to ask you questions about your finances. The main function of the hearing is to ensure that your creditors are allowed representation and for the trustee to determine that your individual case does not constitute an "abuse" of the bankruptcy process. If everything is in order, the trustee will then take charge of your "estate" and a portion of your assets will be sold so that the proceeds can be applied toward paying your debts.

The prospect of seeing your hard-earned valuables being auctioned off may sound intimidating. However, most courts allow Chapter 7 filers to keep most of their property. The U.S. bankruptcy code, a form of federal law, extends a number of property exemptions that disallow creditors from seizing certain items. For one, so long as you haven't recently taken money out of your pension or retirement plan, under federal bankruptcy law these investments are generally off-limits to creditors. If you are collecting life insurance, unemployment or veteran's benefits, or some sort of type of public aid, these sources of income are also exempt.

While no single item can be worth more than $475, federal law also dictates that you are entitled to retain your clothing, furniture, appliances and household goods, providing the combined total doesn't exceed $9,850. As part of a "tools of trade" exemption, you are entitled to keep any equipment, computer, publications or other items relating to your profession, worth up to $1,850. You can also keep your car if the current value doesn't exceed $3,225. There is also a "wild card" exemption that allows you to retain a particular asset or valuables worth up to $925.

If your home is mortgaged to the hilt or you've defaulted on your loan payments, you will probably lose the property regardless of bankruptcy. However, if you own your home in good standing or you've kept up with your house payments, the federal government does include something called a "homestead exemption" that protects properties worth up to $20,200. While this exemption amount may seem minuscule, the amount is intended to reflect the estimated value of your home minus any outstanding loans or mortgages.

Here's where it gets interesting: There is a provision in the bankruptcy code that allows each individual state to formulate its own property exemptions. Some states require that all filers adhere to state guidelines, and others give consumers the choice of choosing either the federal or state exemption package. In many cases, the state exemptions are usually far more generous than those allowed by the federal government. Be sure to research what types of exemptions your state might offer. In the state of Massachusetts, for example, petitioners can keep homes worth up to $300,000. In Maryland, the exempted amount is only $2,500. If you live in Kansas, Florida or Texas, bankruptcy laws disallow the seizure of your home regardless of its value. However, the Bankruptcy Abuse Prevention and Consumer Protection Act, passed in 2005, places new limits on state homestead exemptions.

According to the new law, if you purchased your home within 1,215 days of your bankruptcy filing date, your exemption will be limited to $125,000, regardless of what your state bankruptcy laws might allow. Remember, the worth of a given property is calculated by estimating its current market value and then deducting any debts that may be attached to the property, such as mortgages or loans. If losing your home is your biggest fear, you might want to consider filing for a Chapter 13 bankruptcy, which we will discuss in the next section.

There are also financial obligations that aren't protected by a Chapter 7 proceeding, like student loans, unpaid child support or any type of funds obtained through fraud. In certain limited instances, taxes may be exempted, but only if the debt meets certain conditions. The intricacies of exempting tax debt are a bit beyond the scope of this book, so you may want to consult an attorney or contact your local IRS branch office for guidance.

There is also a good chance that your income may disqualify you from filing for Chapter 7 relief. The 2005 reform legislation we mentioned earlier requires that filers submit to a "means test" in order to quality for Chapter 7 protection. If your monthly earnings in the six-month period prior to your filing are below the median income for the state where you reside, you shouldn't encounter any opposition. However, if your earnings exceed the median income, you will be subjected to an additional test.

The way it works, the bankruptcy court takes your average monthly income and subtracts an IRS-determined expense allowance that provides for your basic necessities, like rent or mortgage payments, utilities, food, etc. Whatever remains is your disposable monthly income (DMI). If your DMI is less than $100, you can still file for Chapter 7 protection.

However, if your remaining disposable income is more than $100 and less than $167.67, multiply this figure by sixty. The outcome of this calculation represents the amount of your earnings that you can apply toward repaying your debts over a five-year period. If the total figure would repay less than 25% of your debts, then you can still file for Chapter 7. For example, let's say you owe your creditors $30,000 and your disposable income is no more than $3,000 over a five year period. Because this is only 10% of the debt, you would still be allowed to file for Chapter 7.

If all goes well, and the bankruptcy court accepts your petition, your court-appointed trustee will sell your non-exempt assets, and the proceeds allocated to your creditors. If your petition is relatively straightforward, in about six months your bankruptcy will be finalized. Most of your debts will be discharged or wiped from the books, and you can look forward to starting over.

Unfortunately, Chapter 7 isn't the best fit for everyone. If your home can't be protected by homestead exemptions, a Chapter 7 filing won't protect you from losing your house. However, you also have the option of "Reaffirmation," which allows you to retain certain types of secured debts. If your creditor consents, you can exclude the properties you wish to keep from the bankruptcy proceedings and continue making your monthly payments, and the creditor will agree to stay any foreclosure proceedings.

While it may end many of your problems, it is worth keeping in mind that bankruptcy is not an entirely pain-free ordeal. Amassing the required paperwork, documentation and other necessary materials will be both tedious and time-consuming. Moreover, your credit rating will plummet, as will your ability to take out loans, obtain credit cards and even move into a new apartment. However, you will be allowed to make a fresh start, and this might be the only realistic way to rebuild your finances and move on with your life.

Filing for Chapter 13 Bankruptcy

IF YOU DON'T QUALIFY FOR CHAPTER 7 RELIEF, YOUR ONLY OTHER option is a Chapter 13 bankruptcy. Although you aren't allowed to discharge your debts like you would in a Chapter 7 proceeding, this type of bankruptcy does allow you to keep your property, and gives you some much-needed breathing space to rebuild your finances. To qualify, your total unsecured debts (credit cards, bills, etc.) must be less than $336,900, and your total secured debts (home and car loans) cannot exceed $1,010,650. You are also prohibited from filing for this type of bankruptcy if you have filed a bankruptcy petition that was dismissed within the last six months. A Chapter 13 bankruptcy also requires a regular source of income.

The key word for this type of bankruptcy is reorganization. You will submit the same documents that are required in a Chapter 7 proceeding (itemized list of debts and assets, "schedule" of income and expenditures, certificate of credit counseling, monthly expenses, etc.) to the bankruptcy court. The filing fee is $239, with an added miscellaneous administrative fee of $35. However, within fifteen days of filing, you are also required to submit a specific plan outlining how you will repay your debts over a designated period of time, which is usually three or five years depending on what the court decides.

Your liabilities will be divided into three categories: priority, secured and unsecured. Priority debts are given the most emphasis by the bankruptcy court, and include taxes and the various expenses paid to the courts as part of the bankruptcy proceeding. Secured claims include such items as homes and cars that allow the creditor to foreclose or repossess the property, and for this reason are given greater weight by the bankruptcy court. Unsecured debt is given the lowest priority, and includes most types of consumer and credit card debt.

Like a Chapter 7 proceeding, approximately a month after your filing date a hearing will be held with your creditors that you will need to attend. You will be placed under oath, and both your court-appointed trustee and your creditors will be allowed to pose questions to you about your repayment plan. To avoid any disputes over your plan, it is often advised that you consult with the trustee for additional guidance.

Regardless of how the bankruptcy court rules on your petition, you must mail in the first installment of your repayment plan at least a month after filing. Your creditors are then notified to submit proof of your debts to the court. If the court approves your plan, you will then be required to allocate a certain percentage of your disposable income to the trustee, who will apply these proceeds to your creditors. Some bankruptcy courts require that this be deducted from your paycheck, so there's a good chance that your human resources department will be notified of your shaky finances.

Like a Chapter 7, a Chapter 13 bankruptcy gives you the benefit of a temporary automatic stay on your debts. If you're behind on your house or car loan, you can use this grace period to catch up on your payments. However, timing is everything, and you must act fast. The law dictates that defaults must be corrected within a short time, which is usually about twelve months.

If you consider a Chapter 13 bankruptcy, be prepared to scale down your lifestyle. The majority of your disposable income will go toward your repayment plan. You will also be prohibited from incurring any further debt and you will lose a great deal of financial freedom, as your trustee has the right to disallow any expenditure that is considered extravagant or non-essential. Unlike a Chapter 7, your remaining debts won't be officially discharged until you've completed your payment plan, which could drag on for a few years. You must also make sure that the plan you submit is workable. Many people fail to keep up with their Chapter 13 payments and find themselves back at square one.

Should you fall behind on your payments, you have a few remaining avenues open to you. For one, you can petition the court for a "hardship discharge" which, if successful, will allow you to discharge some of your debts. However, you must meet three specific requirements by proving that:

- You are not personally responsible for your inability to pay. Examples would include a family illness or job loss.

- You have paid your creditors an approximate amount equal to what they would have received had you liquidated your property in a Chapter 7 proceeding.

- Your financial situation is so precarious you would be unable to maintain even a revised payment plan.

If the court grants the hardship discharge, you will still be responsible for secured debts, such as your car or mortgage payments, but your unsecured debts would be discharged. If this fails, you can either attempt to file a Chapter 7 bankruptcy (which you might now qualify for), or ask for your bankruptcy to be dismissed and hope that you can repay the debts on your own.

Bankrupter Beware

WHILE MODERN BANKRUPTCY LAWS WERE INITIALLY DESIGNED TO assist the debtor, in recent years the pendulum has started to inch back toward the creditor. Along with the provisions we discussed in the sections above, the 2005 Bankruptcy Abuse Prevention and Consumer Protection Act includes a number of additional requirements that you must meet in order to qualify for bankruptcy protections.

For one, take the time to organize your financial documents. Be sure to have copies of your tax returns handy, as you must include a copy of your most recent tax return within a week of your first hearing or your case will be dismissed. If any of your creditors request additional tax returns, the court can demand that you submit tax returns for up to four years prior to filing. You must also provide the court with copies of any paychecks you may have received within two months of filing your petition.

You also need to complete a court-approved credit-counseling course from an approved agency prior to filing for bankruptcy. A certification that you have completed the mandated counseling and a repayment plan must be included with the papers you file with the bankruptcy court. You can undergo counseling either in person, online or over the telephone. A typical session lasts about ninety minutes and will include a comprehensive budget analysis. Additionally, you must also attend a financial planning course after you have filed your petition with the bankruptcy court. If you don't meet these requirements, you may be denied bankruptcy protection.

Creditors can also challenge the discharge of certain debts in a Chapter 7 proceeding. For example, you cannot be shielded from a debt to a creditor of over $500 or more if the expense is deemed to be a "luxury" by the bankruptcy court and the charge is made within three months of filing. If your debts aren't discharged, you could find yourself facing a lawsuit from your creditors. Most people filing for bankruptcy can hardly afford to defend themselves in a civil action, which will give stubborn creditors a powerful incentive to make sure many of your debts are not discharged.

If you find yourself in a situation where bankruptcy may be your only option, keep in mind that it can go very simply or it can be a complex process. If you can afford the expense, consider retaining a bankruptcy lawyer. If you don't have the money for legal fees and must file on your own behalf, take some time to research how the process works.

The book *Surviving Personal Bankruptcy* by Nora Raum, a nationally recognized bankruptcy expert, provides an excellent overview of bankruptcy laws and demystifies the confusing legal jargon found in federal law. Nolo Books (nolo.com) also publishes a number of highly regarded titles detailing how to file for bankruptcy. You can also find valuable information about bankruptcy on the internet at sites like WeFreeDebt.com, and the U.S. Court System also provides some relatively straightforward guidance at uscourts.gov/bankruptcy-courts/bankruptcybasics.html.

When You Don't File

WHILE BANKRUPTCY MAY BE IN YOUR BEST LONG-TERM INTERESTS, that doesn't mean everyone files. You might be strongly averse to turning over personal financial information to the court, allowing a trustee to liquidate your assets or submitting to a court-ordered payment plan. There are some who believe that walking away from one's debts without making an attempt at repaying them is simply unethical. Maybe you hold the belief that the government rarely solves people's problems, and often makes them worse. Whatever the reason, if you are strongly opposed to filing for bankruptcy, you have a few options available to you.

The automatic stay and the peace of mind that comes with living without the constant presence of irate bill collectors is often what makes bankruptcy so attractive to many consumers. However, if this type of harassment is your main concern, and you intend to cover your debts at a future date, bankruptcy isn't the only means of deterring the collection agencies. The Fair Debt Collection Practices Act (FDCPA) was enacted in 1978 to protect debtors from deceptive or abusive practices by collection agencies. While the law primarily applies to third-party creditors (collection agencies), many states have enacted similar laws that prohibit the same practices by second party creditors as well. Be sure to investigate if your state has any existing measures that address collection practices.

If debt collectors are making your life miserable, it's worth knowing that the FDCAP specifically prohibits the following practices:

- Calling during odd hours or making repeated telephone calls to your workplace or residence. According to the law, any call before 8 a.m. or after 9 p.m. is not allowed unless you have given the bill collector permission to do so.

- Contacting a third party who has no financial involvement in the debt, i.e., relatives, neighbors or employers. However, if there is a co-signer, he or she may be contacted.

- Making threats of filing a lawsuit, reporting non-payment to credit reporting agencies, repossession or garnishing wages without any real intent of carrying them out. Debt collectors are only allowed to contact consumers if they plan on any taking any of these actions.

- Contacting you at work if you have specifically forbidden the bill collector to do so.

- Using racial slurs, insults or profane language.

- Making false representations to the debtor, such as posing as an attorney and alleging that a lawsuit has been filed against you, or using stationery intended to look like (or even posing as) an official government or court document.

- Threatening arrest.

- Attempting to coerce collection fees or interest payments from debtors.

- Instituting lawsuits far from the consumer's place of residence.

- Demanding post-dated checks.

- Using false claims to obtain financial information from the debtor, such as posing as someone collecting information for a survey.

Under FDCPA, you are entitled to write to collection agencies and specifically state how you would like to be contacted. If you don't want to be called at home or at work, they will be forced to abide by your request. If you have clearly stated that you don't wish to be called, third-party creditors can only call to inform you that they will be instituting legal proceedings against you. If you find yourself being badgered by unscrupulous bill collectors, you have the right to file suit against any third-party creditor that violates FDCPA, and you can recoup up to $1,000 plus any court costs or attorney fees. Most debt collection agencies are hoping that you are ignorant of your protections under FDCPA. If you want to stop the constant telephone calls, make sure that you know your rights, and be prepared to respond if you think the law has been violated.

If you'd really like to make a good faith effort to clear up your debts without resorting to bankruptcy, you might want to consider contacting your creditors and asking to settle the debts for lesser amounts or possibly setting up a payment plan. While you might not have much luck with some of the larger credit card companies, as most of these institutions profit greatly from exorbitant interest fees, it's worth a try. Likewise, you won't make much headway trying to bargain with a mortgage company over a large, secured debt. However, if you have any debts with local merchants and other creditors, they may not be averse to some sort of settlement or giving you some extra time to repay what you owe. If you're a professional or artisan, you might even consider offering to barter your services in exchange for reduced bills.

You can also check with a consumer credit counseling agency in your area. While some of these organizations are underwritten by credit card companies, and can often make things worse, some of them are very good at advocating for consumers deeply in debt, and (for a fee) they might be able to assist you in reducing your debt load, or at the very least providing a workable payment plan to settle your debts without going into bankruptcy. Be wary, for there are a lot of scams and unscrupulous people out there—try to find a reputable agency in your area.

If you're flat busted, have nothing of value that can be repossessed and you simply don't care, you have the option of walking away from your debts. People with few assets, like a senior citizen who survives on a fixed income, or disabled or unemployed individuals, are "judgment proof," and few creditors will institute legal proceedings against them, as both their income and the few assets they own are exempted from being taken by creditors. In the majority of cases, the debts are simply written off. While your credit rating may take a beating, you will at least avoid the hassle of a bankruptcy, and if your luck improves, you might be able to repay your debts at a later time and clean up your credit history.

Obviously, the wisest course of action is to make preparations now so that you can avoid bankruptcy altogether. Indeed, there is a veritable cottage industry of credit counseling firms, bankruptcy attorneys, accountants and others who have turned consumer insolvency into a thriving cottage industry, and would like nothing better than to profit from economic downturn.

As advised in a previous chapter, your safest course of action in these uncertain times is to cut back on wasteful expenses, keep to a strict budget and live as frugally as you can. Unfortunately, when your options are limited, bankruptcy may prove to be your wisest choice. •

Notes

1   Zibel, Alan. "Personal Bankruptcy Filings Rise 40%," Associated Press, January 4, 2008.

2   Weston, Liz Pulliam. "Why Going Broke Is a Fact of Life in America," MSN Money, June 30, 2004.

3   Kusmer, Kenneth L. *Down and Out, On the Road: The Homeless in American History*, (New York: Oxford, 2002). p. 13.

CHAPTER 5

IN CASE OF EMERGENCY
THE RESILIENT HOME

In Case of Emergency: The Resilient Home

AT A TIME WHEN MOST OF US ARE FOCUSED ON OUR PERSONAL financial situation and the nation's economic health, preparedness may not be high on the list of priorities. Nevertheless, we cannot ignore the fact that America's financial woes could impact critical government services. Indeed, long before the current crisis ever materialized, security expert Stephen E. Flynn was warning in the March 2008 issue of *Foreign Affairs* that "Most city and state public health and emergency management departments are not funded to carry out even their routine work."[1]

The situation will likely worsen as federal, state and municipal governments contend with rising unemployment, shrinking tax revenues and funding cuts. According to a December 2008 report issued by Trust for America's Health (TFAH), a non-profit that monitors public health programs and emergency services, the ongoing financial crisis could undermine the nation's ability to respond to everything from natural disasters to medical emergencies. "The 25% cut in federal support to protect Americans from diseases, disasters and bioterrorism is already hurting state response capabilities," asserts TFAH Executive Director Jeff Levi. "The cuts to state budgets in the next few years could lead to a disaster for the nation's disaster preparedness."[2]

The shocking ineptitude that characterized official relief efforts throughout the 2005 Hurricane Katrina disaster was a discomforting reminder that we cannot always rely on the government when events take a turn for the worst. It's often unsettling to contemplate worst-case scenarios. However, we cannot ignore the fact that America's crumbling and long-neglected infrastructure, a dysfunctional and often secretive emergency management bureaucracy, and the large populations residing in high-risk areas have left us increasingly vulnerable to extreme weather events and any number of cascading system failures, from blackouts to food and water shortages.

Complacency is simply no longer an option. For far too long we've been lulled into a false sense of security by paternalistic public officials who have actively encouraged the prevailing belief that only "cranks" and "paranoids" concern themselves with survival planning. Fortunately, it's not too late to start sharpening your survival skills and increasing your preparedness.

Water: Lifeblood of Survival

WE DISCUSSED THE IMPORTANCE OF SETTING UP A FOOD STORAGE cache in a previous chapter, and it is hoped that you will set aside at least a seven-day supply of emergency rations. It is also critically important that you have an emergency water supply on hand. No matter how big your food stash, if you run out of water, you simply won't survive. We can go without food for weeks, but people forced to go without water can perish in as few as three days. United Nations experts recommend, as an absolute rock bottom minimum, at least seven liters (or slightly under two gallons) per person per day for both drinking and washing.[3] For daily hydration alone, estimates range from two quarts to a gallon of drinking water every day. Children, pregnant women, the infirm and people who reside in hot weather regions are advised to drink at least a gallon a day, so be sure you have set aside adequate reserves.

There are additional factors that will also add to your water intake. As we obtain much of our daily fluid requirements through the food we eat, if forced to survive on limited rations for your meals, you will need to make up the difference by ingesting more water. Your level of exertion will also play a role in how much water you may require each day. Be aware that dehydration is a constant threat in survival-threatened situations. An effective way to ensure you are properly hydrated is to closely monitor your daily urine. If you are drinking enough water, your urine stream will be clear. If it is cloudy, colored or odorous, that's a good indication that you aren't sufficiently hydrated. Tempting as it might be, avoid drinking alcohol or caffeine in situations when your water is limited. Both of these fluids have diuretic properties that will only make you more dehydrated, and thus require additional precious water.

Water Storage

WHEN CONTEMPLATING WATER STORAGE OPTIONS, A TYPICAL FIRST impulse is to rush down to the supermarket and buy several cases of prepackaged bottled water. However, you must remember that this strategy poses a couple of underlying problems. Most bottled water comes in containers made from PVC plastic that, if exposed to heat, may become unhealthy to drink. To increase the flexibility of the plastic, PVC manufacturers often rely on a group of chemicals known as phthalates, which may have adverse health consequences. Additionally, although most manufacturers claim that bottled water has an indefinite shelf life, the water may become increasingly stale and unpalatable over time.

However, if your home or apartment has a sizable storage area that is cool, dark and away from any and all non-food chemicals like solvents, gasoline and paint thinners, stockpiling bottled water might be the easiest course to take. Although it might be an added expense, it would be a good idea to rotate your water supply on a regular basis in order to ensure the freshness of your emergency provisions. You must also make sure that your water bottles remain sealed and unopened, as otherwise they may become inundated with bacteria.

If you simply don't have the space to stack cases of bottled water, or you lack a cool, dry area, water mats may be an option. A company called Aquaflex (Aquaflex.net) supplies home water storage units that are constructed for ease of use and storage capability. While the larger mats, which hold hundreds of gallons, can be stored under your bed, you can also stagger several smaller thirty-gallon mats throughout your home or apartment, or in a closet or bathroom. Prices range from just under $70 for a 3' x 3' 30-gallon water mat, to just over $300 for a 4.5' x 12' model that holds 300 gallons.

When filled, the larger-sized mats will likely weigh hundreds of pounds, so if you live in an apartment building, it is advised that you check with your landlord to ensure that your floors will be able to handle the additional weight. If not, you can still buy a series of smaller mats that may prove easier to transport. The more affordable mats are constructed out of food-grade copolymer. However, if you spring for the expensive Aquatank II model, your water will be protected by a rugged, polyurethane-coated vinyl that will ensure durability and help avoid accidental punctures. Nevertheless, if you obtain a water mat, it's still a good idea to place it in a safe, out-of-the-way location to avoid any possible mishaps or accidents, like pets chewing on the mat. Wrapping your mat in a tarp is also a good idea. If you choose to deploy water mats, perhaps the most important benefit is that you can frequently refresh your existing water and reserves and be sure of a clean and palatable water source should disaster strike.

Using plastic drums is another popular water storage method. These leak-proof containers come in a variety of sizes, ranging from one to over fifty-five gallons. The larger models usually come with a hand pump for ease of use. If you lack the space for the bigger containers, you can always buy units in the ten- to fifteen-gallon range and scatter them throughout your home or apartment. Before buying, make sure that the barrels are made of high-density polyethylene (HDPE) plastic, which is specifically approved by the Food and Drug Administration for food and water storage. As long as your containers are constructed of this material, you won't have to worry about any chemicals leaching into your water supply. Before filling the barrels with water, take the time to thoroughly clean each container with dishwashing soap and water, and rinse thoroughly so that there isn't any residual soap.

If you plan on storing water in plastic containers, keep them in a cool, dark place and be sure that your water reserves are far away from any toxic substances or chemicals, and that they have tight, sealable lids. Plastic water containers can usually be found at most camping and military surplus stores. If you prefer to shop online, SurvivalUnlimited.com offers a very good selection. You can also stash some additional water in your freezer using sealable Ziploc bags. Not only will you have a good extra supply of water, but also, should your power go out, the frozen water might keep your foods from perishing during a temporary blackout.

So long as you replace your emergency water supply on a regular basis, you needn't worry about using bleach and other chemicals to disinfect your reserves. According to the American Red Cross, treating your water with bleach is both "superfluous and unnecessary" if your tap water "is treated commercially by a water treatment utility."[4] Be sure to check with the water management agency that serves your area to make sure that your tap water is properly treated. If not, you can always purchase chemically treated water through commercial suppliers, or recycle your water reserves on a more frequent basis.

Emergency Water Sources

MURPHY'S LAW TELLS US THAT EVEN THE MOST DETAILED PLANNING can often fall victim to unforeseen circumstances. No one can predict the future, and for any number of reasons you may be required to obtain your water from non-traditional sources. For example, suppose you are left without water during an unexpected heat wave. Because of the extreme heat, you may be forced to consume additional water that could deplete your existing reserves. Fortunately, nature has endowed us with three sources of water that can be used in an emergency situation: rainwater, surface water and groundwater.

In many instances, rainwater won't be the most dependable source. If you find yourself in a survival-threatened situation in the middle of summer, in most of the country your chances of collecting adequate rainwater are going to be slim to none. However, in other seasons, or in parts of the country that experience a great deal of rainfall, setting up a water collection system will greatly enhance your existing reserves. Getting down to basics, each square yard of your catchment area will yield approximately 6.4 gallons per inch of rainfall.[5]

Companies like Aquabarrel (aquabarrel.com) and Spruce Creek (sprucecreekrainsaver.com) offer safe and efficient rainwater barrels that can be purchased online. You can also construct your own using food-grade plastic containers. Natural Rain Water (naturalrainwater.com) has some tips and suggestions on how to construct your own rain barrel. If you plan on harvesting rainwater, it's a good idea to make the same preparations you would make if you were using the containers for water storage. If you'd like some tips on how to efficiently collect rainwater, Harvest H2O (harvesth2o.com) is an excellent resource.

Surface water can be found in ponds, rivers and streams that may or may not be easily accessible to readers who reside in overdeveloped urban areas. Moreover, in America's cities surface water will likely be greatly problematic, as it is very likely that these water sources could be contaminated by pollution, litter, waste or industrial chemicals infecting the groundwater that feeds into rivers and streams. Look for telltale signs of possible contamination, such as the presence of feces (animal or otherwise), clouded water or a strong smell. If you're simply not sure, it might be a good idea to move on and find a more suitable place. Take the time to locate and identify any possible surface water in your area, as it may come in handy in an emergency.

Groundwater can be found below the surface of the earth, and is usually harvested by digging wells. Because the earth serves as a natural source of filtration, subterranean water is considered one of the safer forms of water in an emergency situation. Unfortunately, due to the abundance of concrete in most urban settings and over-utilization of existing water sources, this may prove to be quite a challenge for urban dwellers. To get a general idea of where you might find sources of subterranean water, closely examine the water table for your area, which can usually be obtained through your city planning department. This is important, because digging a well is a laborious chore under any circumstances, so in a survival-threatened situation you want to make sure your efforts will pay off.

Grassy areas near rivers and ponds usually contain groundwater. When looking for possible sites, it's usually a good sign if there is an abundance of green vegetation. Should you find a possible source of groundwater, keep in mind that digging a well is considered a two-person job, and requires a shovel, pickaxe, a large number of bricks, mortar, a good-sized bucket, a collection of smaller-sized rocks (to line the bottom) and a rope. For more detailed information about well construction, safety and maintenance, it is highly advised you visit the web page for Lifewater Canada (lifewater.ca) a non-profit that has an invaluable well-digging tutorial posted online.

In a pinch, you can also harvest some emergency water from a few sources inside your home or apartment. Even if your water has been shut off, there will likely be additional water in your pipes. Locate and close the main water valve to your home, as this will keep the water trapped inside your pipes. To drain the water, turn off your water heater, locate the highest faucet in your home and let air into the pipes by turning it on full blast. You can then drain water from the lowest faucet. Be sure to have a clean, food-grade container to store the water in.

Your hot water heater may also hold between twenty and eighty gallons of water. To drain the tank, you will first need to turn off the electricity or gas. Switch the circuit breaker to the "off" position or close the gas valve. To get the water flowing, turn on a hot water faucet and then open the drain, which is located at the bottom of the tank. To make it easier, you can connect a garden hose to the bottom of the tank and use a barrel or several containers to store the water. Before draining, make sure you've given the water time to cool off or you could be accidentally scalded. If you'd like further guidance on how to perform this operation, consult with your building superintendent, landlord or the company that services your water heater.

It might be somewhat unsavory, but in a dire emergency, the water stored in the reservoir tank (as opposed to the bowl) of your toilet can be used for drinking water. You may wish to disinfect prior to drinking (we'll discuss purification in the next section). You can also use the water in ice cube trays and the juices in canned goods in a dire emergency. Even if it's a crisis situation, never drink water from swimming pools, radiators or waterbeds.

Purification

ANY SURFACE WATER, RAINWATER OR GROUNDWATER SHOULD BE purified to eliminate any existing pathogens, viruses or contaminants. If you drink unsafe water you run the risk of contracting a number of waterborne illnesses, like *E. coli,* cholera and salmonella. Viruses like Hepatitis A, and protozoa like *Giardia* and *Cryptosporidium* can also be present in water, as well as a number of pesticides and other industrial chemicals. You simply don't want to run this risk, no matter how thirsty you might be.

The most common purification method is simply boiling the water for a good five minutes (tack on an extra minute for every 1,000 feet you are above sea level). Once the water cools down and settles, let it sit for a short while and then pour the water into a separate clean, food-grade container. If you are facing an emergency situation, household Clorox bleach can also be used. Add at least eight, and no more than twelve, drops of bleach to each gallon of water. Let the water stand for a half hour and transfer to a clean, sterilized container. If you've added the bleach correctly, the water should give off a slight odor of chlorine. If not, add a few more drops of bleach and repeat the process. When storing your survival gear, it might be a good idea to stock up on extra bleach (don't buy the lemon-scented kind, it's not adequate for purification) and tape a medicine dropper to your bleach bottles so that you can properly measure out each dose.

If you're concerned about taste and want to ensure that your water is clean and free of bacteria and contaminants, it is highly recommended that you invest in a high-quality water filter. While popular water filters like PUR and Brita will filter out most contaminants, these types of filters may not be capable of eliminating all impurities. If you are looking for a comprehensive water purification system, it may be a bit pricey at $200 and up, but Berkey Filters (berkeyfilters.com) offers an amazing portable filtration system capable of eliminating pathogens, bacteria, cysts, herbicides, pesticides, heavy metals and other impurities. If you want to be extra certain that you are drinking clean water, this is a worthwhile investment.

Sanitation

GOOD HEALTH WILL BE ONE OF YOUR PRIMARY ASSETS IN A CRISIS, so you must make every effort to maintain a clean, germ-free environment. If you've just survived a natural disaster or you're contending with a food or water shortage, these situations will be inherently stressful and this could compromise your immune system. It is also highly likely that you will be eating far less than usual, and the possible threat of malnutrition will leave you even more susceptible to falling ill. Even if your water is scarce, try to maintain good hygiene habits. Skin infections are easy to develop, so be sure to wash your hands regularly and, at the very least, try to give yourself a daily sponge bath or scrub yourself with a wet towel. Be sure to use an antibacterial soap. If water is at a premium, you also have the option of lightly daubing your body with a clean towel or rag dipped in rubbing alcohol, aftershave, liquor or any liquid containing alcohol. Try to clean your towel, sponge or rag after each use.

Poor sanitation is another looming threat. According to the United Nations, millions of people perish from illnesses every year that can be directly linked to poorly managed, unsterile or non-existent bathroom facilities.[6] When sanitation is compromised, there is usually a high rate of cholera, diarrhea, respiratory infection, worms and a host of other medical conditions. While it is comforting to believe that this simply doesn't happen in advanced countries, take a moment to remember the disturbing reports of stranded evacuees forced to sleep next to piles of human waste in New Orleans after Hurricane Katrina.

If you are lucky, you will still have the option of using your existing toilet facility. Even if the water has been turned off, so long as your local sewer system is intact, you can still use your toilet. However, instead of flushing, pour a five-gallon bucket or other large container of water into the bowl; this should provide a sufficient flush for your waste. If you don't have enough water in your provisions for this method, you can still use your toilet. Drain the water from the bowl and affix or tape a sturdy plastic bag (the kind with twist-ties if possible) to the underside of your toilet seat. When the bag is approximately half full, add disinfectant and seal it off with the twist-ties, a piece of tape or some twine. Ten parts water to one part bleach is usually recommended for a disinfectant. While the idea of crapping in a plastic bag may sound strange, you will at least have some privacy, and being able to use a toilet may prove more psychologically comforting than crouching over a hole in the ground or squatting over a bucket.

Disposing of human waste is not an enviable chore, and you must avoid the temptation to bury your foul-smelling bags in the ground. Not only will this draw disease-carrying insects, but there's also a strong possibility that you could pollute your local groundwater supply. Try setting aside a disinfected trash can for this purpose. Make sure that your container is lined with a couple of sturdy trash bags and has a secure lid. Place your tightly sealed bags in the can and add disinfectant. Remember to wear gloves when possible. If you're worried about the smell, especially in hot weather, kitty litter does a great job of neutralizing fecal odors. Be sure to fortify your waste disposal can so that it won't be easily knocked over, and stock up on pre-moistened antibacterial wipes at your local drug store so that you can ensure your hands are properly cleaned after depositing a load in your waste can.

In Darkness

BLACKOUTS HAVE BECOME INCREASINGLY COMMON IN RECENT YEARS, and the prospect of being plunged into complete darkness is a contingency that shouldn't go ignored. Thanks to recent innovations in technology, achieving a modicum of comfort amidst a total system failure isn't an insurmountable obstacle. Let's begin with lighting.

Most camping stores carry a number of emergency hand-crank LED lanterns that can make a major difference in a blackout situation. Most run in the $20–30 range, and you can place one in each room of your home or apartment. For sheer simplicity, these can't be beat. They don't require batteries or bulbs, and provide twenty minutes of lighting for every three minutes they are cranked. The majority of these products come with an outlet, so you have the option of charging them prior to use if you find the hand-cranking tedious. Solar-powered lamps are a bit more expensive, but are also reliable and well worth the cost. Global Marketing Technologies (gmtems.com) offers a wide array of solar rechargeable lanterns and other products for under $100, which can provide high-quality illumination for hours.

Candles, LED and solar-powered flashlights, headlamps and the chemical light sticks used by campers and military personnel are all good options, and can be purchased at any camping or military supply store. Remember, if you should experience a power outage, wait until your eyes adjust to the darkness before attempting to locate your emergency lighting supplies. It's also a good idea to place luminescent stickers on your lanterns and flashlights so that you won't accidentally injure yourself looking for them in the dark. If you plan on relying on battery-powered flashlights and lanterns, be sure to use rechargeable batteries and, if possible, purchase a solar-powered battery charger to ensure that you can charge your batteries even if the grid is down.

While we will address alternate power sources and generators in greater detail in another chapter, if you have limited space and want to ensure that you'll be able to run your laptop, charge your cell phone and carry out other minor tasks in an emergency, consider investing in a small-sized portable backup generator. For just under $100, Duracell's Powerpack 600 (duracell.com) can be charged from any household AC outlet or automobile DC or cigarette lighter outlet. The unit is powered by a 28-amp battery that is tied to a power inverter capable of providing 600 watts to the Powerpack's three electrical outlets. The unit comes with an AM/FM radio, a high-powered emergency light and jumper cables should the unit be needed in a roadside emergency. While it may not be able to power some of your bigger appliances, so long as you keep it regularly charged, the 600 can at least handle some of your day-to-day electrical needs in a blackout situation.

Home Security

PREPAREDNESS REQUIRES A PLAN FOR EVERY EVENTUALITY, AND YOU shouldn't ignore the possibility that the current economic crisis could lead to a serious rise in crime. Most self-defense experts agree that a well-protected home is by far the first and foremost line of defense against theft or robbery. It's a well-known fact that the majority of criminals tend to focus on easy targets. Take a good look at your home or apartment and identify and fortify the various weak points that would allow an intruder to gain easy access to your home. Make sure that windows are secure and your front door has a theft-proof deadbolt lock. Consider obtaining a watchdog or installing an alarm system. You can also set up a low-cost webcam and post signs that all activity is being recorded.

Your neighbors can also provide additional eyes and ears. Discuss your security precautions with them and promise to watch their home or apartment if they'll keep an eye on your residence. As thieves tend to operate in the darkness, make sure that the area outside your home is well lit. Many home invasion robberies begin with a simple knock at the door, so try to devise a neutral area where you can speak with evening callers that doesn't involve opening your front door. If you have a balcony or a window that will allow you to converse, that may be your safest option.

Your primary goal is to ensure that your typical burglar will encounter several obstacles before he or she can even think of entering your home. In terms of home security, the threat of carjacking is another danger you must consider. Stay on the alert whenever you are driving, and particularly when stepping into or getting out of your vehicle. These are the times when you are at your most vulnerable. Always be wary of strangers loitering nearby, and scan the inside of the car to make sure no one may be crouching in the back seat. After you step inside, immediately lock all doors. If you detect that someone is following you, never stop. Consider honking your horn to draw attention and proceeding to somewhere safe, like a police station or well-lit store entrance where security personnel will be nearby.

An additional deterrent against a carjacking or robbery is a firearm. If you live in a state where concealed weapons permits are allowed, consider obtaining one and carrying a weapon. Although the government and the media rarely broadcast this well-known truism, most violent criminals fear armed citizens more than they do police, and hundreds of thousands of people successfully use firearms in self-defense each year. According to one study by criminologists Gary Kleck and Mark Gertz, the majority of armed self-defense encounters rarely involve firing the weapon, as merely brandishing a firearm is one of the most effective deterrents to crime—"[Crime] victims who resist by using guns or other weapons are less likely to be injured compared to victims who do not resist or to those who resist without weapons."[7]

However, if you make the decision to arm yourself, don't take the matter lightly. Owning and operating a firearm is a serious responsibility, and safety should be your utmost priority. Never resort to a gun unless you truly believe your own or someone else's life is truly in danger and it's your only available option. Never playfully point your weapon at people, dry fire or carelessly leave your weapons out in plain sight. If you have children or frequent visitors, a trigger lock or gun safe might be an option worth considering. Be sure to visit your local pistol range or contact your nearest National Rifle Association chapter, as either will provide information about safety courses, weapons training and educational materials.

Make sure your weapon is regularly cleaned and oiled, and spend some time on the shooting range so that loading and firing become second nature. For home defense, most experts recommend a twelve-gauge shotgun and a pistol as a backup. As semi-automatics have a tendency to jam, a revolver might be your best choice for a sidearm for ease of use and reliability.

Should you take a self-defense training course? Expert opinion varies. Many of the elaborate martial arts techniques currently being taught are next to worthless against an armed assailant, and may take years to master. However, on the positive side, many of these courses teach students to "think like a warrior" by developing a heightened sense of awareness and ability to detect signs of possible danger. These are invaluable skills to possess should you find yourself in danger.

The level of security you choose for your home is dependent upon a number of factors, such as your personal beliefs about violence, the region where you live and your current finances, to name just a few. Whatever you decide, don't let your concerns about crime become an obsession. When you're living in constant fear, you've already lost. By all means take adequate precautions and stay alert, but constantly worrying about the unknown isn't going to make you any safer.

Street Strategies

WHILE YOU CAN TAKE PRECAUTIONS TO CRIME-PROOF YOUR HOUSE or apartment, when you go out in public you will need to adopt similar measures to ensure your safety. If concealed weapons permits are allowed in your area, this might be a consideration. However, this needn't be your only line of defense. There are also some simple, common sense precautions that may help you avoid falling victim to violent crime:

• Always trust your instincts. We each have a sixth sense that tells us when danger is close by. Pay close attention to these internal cues. If someone suspicious-looking is approaching you, let your instincts dictate whether it would be safer to cross to the other side of the street, or a different street altogether.

• Walk with a steady, confident step and avoid unnecessary conversation with strangers. Most street robberies begin with a simple question such as "Can I have a light?" or "Do you have a quarter?" While you dig in your pocket, an accomplice or your interlocutor will brandish a weapon. Remember, not all random conversations are benign. Someone could be closely observing you as a possible victim. When you don't feel safe, sometimes being friendly is a luxury you can't afford.

• In a high-crime, urban setting, never allow yourself to be distracted. If you are walking down the street, to your car or to work, don't make the mistake of gabbing on your cell phone, listening to your iPod, reading or any other activity that will keep you from focusing on your surroundings. You may not know it, but someone may be watching you, and your absent-minded behavior gives a would-be robber both the element of surprise and a tactical edge.

• Never be ostentatious with your money. Keep a few small bills in your front pocket for purchases and avoid using your wallet when you can. Flashing a wad of bills or a bulging wallet is never a good idea under any circumstance, and will only draw unwelcome attention.

• If someone grabs your purse, messenger bag, backpack or laptop, simply let them take it. People have died fighting over a few worthless items in a handbag. Always remember, your possessions can be replaced—your life can't.

• When you can, avoid walking by yourself in risky urban settings. Most street criminals prefer to go after a lone individual who can be easily cornered. The larger your group, the less likely you will be attacked or robbed. Even in groups, avoid walking down dark streets or taking shortcuts through rundown neighborhoods. Stay in well-lit areas when possible. Make sure that at least a few people know where you are going and when you plan on returning home.

• Always carry your cellular phone and make sure it is fully charged. The ability to make a call for assistance in an emergency could save your life. Make sure you have it with you at all times.

• Avoid using ATMs in dangerous areas. If it's an emergency, you may be better off paying an additional fee to use a cash machine in a safe location like a 7-Eleven or supermarket. Many police stations now have ATMs—using one might be a good idea if you're worried about crime.

• If you use public transportation, stay alert at all times. Pay close attention to any suspicious-looking individuals you might encounter. If someone getting off on your stop looks threatening, consider an alternate stop in a well-lit area.

Hopefully, taking appropriate precautions will keep you out of danger. However, if someone approaches you wielding a firearm and demanding money, you will likely be dealing with a desperate (and possibly unstable) individual who is impervious to reason and focused on one goal: taking your money. Do not become defiant, angry or insulting, as this will only serve to escalate the encounter. Your life is far too valuable to risk over a couple dollars, a few credit cards or a wristwatch. If there is an avenue of escape, consider throwing down your valuable items several feet away and then running away as fast as you can. Make no mistake—if your primary focus is survival, sometimes even the most battle-hardened warrior must know when to walk (or run) away.

Unfortunately, there are some criminals who aren't willing to let you walk away after taking your money. This is when even the most devoted pacifist will need to consider self-defense measures. Statistics indicate that when an individual is led away from the scene of an initial crime, the chance of surviving becomes increasingly unlikely. Maybe the gunman wants you to take him to ATM so you can withdraw additional funds, or he merely wants you to drive him to a friend's house. Whatever the excuse, your life may be in serious danger.

This is when the ability to defend your life will be crucial. Although carrying a concealed weapon is a crime in many locales, it may be worth your while to investigate what sorts of weapons can be legally carried in your area. If you cannot carry a firearm, you may have the option of deploying pepper spray, mace, a Taser or a stun gun. If you are considering a self-defense course, consider taking a realistic "street-level" class that specializes in teaching simple and effective defensive blows that will temporarily immobilize an attacker. Most experts recommend you drive the heel of your hand into the bridge of your assailant's nose, dig your fingers into his eyes or violently chop at your assailant's windpipe.

If you are serious about defending yourself, don't be half-hearted. Stay in tip-top physical shape so that you can run fast, or use every ounce of strength to deliver a crushing blow. Whether you wish to use a firearm, pepper spray, mace or even a flashlight, make sure that you have practiced to the point that the most basic moves have become second nature. In an absolute worst-case scenario, your life may depend on it. Hopefully, if you take the proper precautions, it won't ever come to that.

Survival on the Run

When making your preparations, keep in mind the possibility that you may be forced to evacuate your home or apartment on very short notice, for any number of reasons. You may one day face an impending hurricane or tornado, encroaching brush fires, a severe earthquake or you may just be unlucky and find yourself locked out of your home or apartment due to foreclosure or non-payment of rent. Consider putting together what survivalists call a "Bug Out Bag" (BOB)—you never know when it might come in handy.

Begin by purchasing a large backpack or military-style duffel bag at a sporting goods or camping store. Your primary aim is to be able to survive for up to seventy-two hours or more without assistance. A typical BOB should contain the following items:

Water: Consider packing at least a three-day supply or more. At a bare minimum, set aside at least one gallon of water per person, per day. The Red Cross recommends that you change your stored water every six months. Be sure to keep the water in durable plastic containers.

Food: Pack a three-day supply of non-perishable food that can be prepared at a moment's notice without requiring any cooking or adding water. You might pack some dried fruit, beef jerky, nuts or military-issue MREs. Include an assortment of vitamins to beef up your daily intake of nutrients. The Red Cross recommends that you include a few "comfort foods" like candy bars or potato chips.

Shelter: You can pick up a lightweight emergency tube tent at most camping stores for under $10. They can be assembled in minutes and can also double as a sheet or tarp.

Light: Glow sticks, a hand-powered crank lantern or a rechargeable flashlight will prove vital if you are forced to hike in the dark or camp in the open air.

First Aid Kit: A good emergency first aid kit will include various bandages, gauze, antiseptic and germicidal wipes, latex gloves, rolls of adhesive tape, ointments, cold packs, scissors, face masks, aspirin, scissors, tweezers and a breathing device to aid CPR.

Self-Defense: If you can, carry a firearm and some extra ammunition. If this is not allowed in your state, consider purchasing some pepper spray or mace as a self-defense precaution.

Miscellaneous: Be sure to include a map of your region, an extra cellular phone or laptop, a hand crank- or battery-operated radio, emergency money, pliers and other tools, a signaling mirror, tape, waterproof matches and disposable lighter, compass, aluminum foil, mess kits, writing utensils, needle and thread, buckets, disinfectant and plastic bags for sanitation, sleeping bags, warm-weather clothing, portable stove and fuel, and a watertight plastic envelope to keep your will, the deed to your house and other vital documents.

These are just some of the basics. Contact your local Red Cross chapter for additional materials on preparing for short-term disaster survival. Once you've assembled your BOB, get used to hiking with it. If it's too heavy, you can either break it down into two smaller bags or consider stripping down your supplies to the bare essentials: food, shelter, water and a few additional items. You can also experiment with a variety of backpacks. Many of the more advanced models available at camping stores allow for a greater distribution of weight and provide additional support for the back and shoulders.

Put together a checklist of the contents of your BOB and practice finding the exact location of each item so that it becomes second nature. Who knows? You may need to pull out a pair of pliers in the dark during a howling rainstorm. Consider placing a similar bag of survival items in your vehicle or at your workplace.

Networked Survival

WHEN RUNAWAY WILDFIRES RAGED THROUGH MALIBU, CALIFORNIA IN 2007, many residents of the popular beach community were forced to evacuate their homes. While information-starved homeowners anxiously waited for news, the local news media wasted precious time obsessing over the plight of a handful of celebrity homes, and traditional emergency services issued hopelessly outdated bulletins. In response, a few resourceful homeowners took to the airwaves. "I knew that a lot of my less savvy friends were having problems getting real information from the news, so I just soaked up as much as I could from the internet and regurgitated it through text messages, instant messaging, Twitter and my blog," a resident later recalled.[8]

The age of social media had arrived. By uploading photos to the internet, transmitting news items via instant message programs, posting to blogs and

ALAMEDA FREE LIBRARY

social networking sites, and using online maps, Malibu's displaced but resilient evacuees were often better informed than the local news networks. According to *New Scientist*, those plugged into the closely-knit social network "were able to gather and disseminate information on, for example, the progress of the fire, the location of evacuation areas and shelters, and which schools and businesses were closed."[9]

This groundbreaking citizen initiative is now being studied by academics that believe that "micro-blogging" sites like Twitter, which integrate blogging, text messaging and social networking into one effective package, have important applications in disaster management. The ability to send and receive up-to-the-minute information in any given situation is a vital survival tool that is well worth examining.

If you're worried about staying informed or maintaining contact with friends and family members during a natural disaster or personal emergency, consider setting up an account with Twitter.com, which will allow you to both track recent news developments in your community and provide moment-by-moment updates of your whereabouts and safety—which could prove vital in a desperate situation. Twitter also allows you to plug into up-to-the-minute news threads in your area. Ning.com is another effective communications tool that allows you to create your own social networking site in seconds.

What occurred in Malibu illustrates how survivors can utilize recent advances in communications technology. When disaster strikes, we often need to react to rapidly changing conditions and require a reliable information stream untainted by the political and institutional biases that sometimes creep into government and media reporting of issues critical to the public. Access to a diverse, well-established network of like-minded individuals residing in your area is a critical survival asset you shouldn't ignore. •

Notes

1   Flynn, Stephen E. "America the Resilient," *Foreign Affairs*, March/April 2008. vol. 87, no. 2, p. 3.

2   Trust for America's Health. "Ready or Not 2008: Protecting the Public's Health from Disaster, Disease and Bioterrorism," December 2008.

3   Cited in McBay, Aric. *Peak Oil Survival: Preparation for Life After Gridcrash*, (Lyons Press: Connecticut, 2006) p. 3.

4   American Red Cross Fact Sheet, "Water Storage Before Disaster Strikes," www.greaterkzooredcross.org/disaster/wtrbfor.pdf

5   McBay, p. 8.

6   United Nations Fact Sheet, "Sanitation Is Vital for Human Health," January 2008. esa.un.org/iys/docs/1%20fact-sheet_health.pdf

7   Kleck, Gary and Mark Gertz. "Armed Resistance to Crime: The Prevalence and Nature of Self-Defense With a Gun," *Journal of Criminal Law and Criminology*, Northwestern University School of Law. 1995. vol. 86, no. 1.

8   Palmer, Jason. "Emergency 2.0 is Coming to a Website Near You," *New Scientist*, May 2, 2008. no. 2654.

9   Ibid.

CHAPTER 6

RETURN TO SIMPLICITY
RETREAT OPTIONS

Return to Simplicity: Retreat Options

THE IDEA OF TURNING BACK THE CLOCK AND ADOPTING A SIMPLER, more sustainable lifestyle seems to captivate the public imagination during historic periods of financial uncertainty. Throughout the Great Depression, economic theorist Dr. Ralph Borsodi convinced thousands of urban dwellers to migrate to the nation's rural areas and take up farming. Decades later, amidst an unpopular war in Vietnam, growing concerns about pollution, and a slumping economy, a great many disaffected suburbanites sought refuge in country living.

Between 1970 and 1976, an estimated four million Americans decamped to the nation's small towns and farming communities, many as part of a grass-roots "Back to the Land" movement that began in the late 1960s.[1] While this innovative social experiment may have resulted in more wrecked marriages than thriving homesteads, its legacy of organic agriculture, self-sufficiency and a reverence for nature has retained an enduring appeal. Indeed, these pioneering efforts are taking on a new relevance as individuals rethink modern life in light of the nation's ongoing financial woes.

Leaving the City

PERHAPS YOU MAY BE INTERESTED IN RETRACING THE FOOTSTEPS OF your Nixon-era predecessors and retreating to the country to set up a modern homestead. There's no denying that leaving the city or suburbs behind and staking out a new existence in a small town or farming community will put you in a far better position to contend with the current economic crisis. Access to fresh water and open space to grow your own produce and raise livestock are a good form of insurance against inflated food prices or the possibility that you may run short of money. The cost of living is also significantly less in the country.

ENVISIONING COLLAPSE: AN INTERVIEW WITH CLAIRE WOLFE

Claire Wolfe is the author of *The Freedom Outlaw's Handbook: 179 Things to Do 'Til the Revolution* and *I Am Not a Number!* published by Paladin Press. She is the co-author of *The State vs. the People* and the young-adult novel *Rebel Fire: Out of the Gray Zone.* Her online writings can be found at backwoodshome.com or billstclair.com/theclairefiles.com/mirror.html.

....

Q: *What sort of country do you envision the U.S. becoming in the next five years? Ten years? Twenty years?*

CW: Let me turn this question sideways, a bit.

Ever since the last thin link between paper currency and precious metals was severed (and that was back in the Nixon administration), I've been expecting hyperinflation or some other form of monetary and social collapse. I shared the survivalist vision of angry mobs looting dying cities, then rampaging into the countryside—yadda yadda yadda.

I shouldn't make light of that vision, because it could still happen, and I think that on a limited basis, it will happen at some times, in some places.

But after thirty-five years of expecting it, I've begun to feel rather like an adherent of one of those religions whose members confidently expect the world to end on Tuesday, November 16 at 8:43 Eastern Standard Time. So they all gather on a hilltop in Nebraska to await... and await... and await... the return of Jesus.

Then, oops. Sorry, we miscalculated. The world is actually going to end on Friday, March 3 at 6:45 a.m.

However, you must keep in mind that operating a self-sustaining farm will involve hard work and single-minded dedication. Individuals who possess a strong work ethic and serious commitment to living a more earth-centered life will have a far better chance of making the transition to an agrarian lifestyle. Your temperament should also guide your decision. If you're the contemplative type that enjoys quiet, dislikes crowds and looks forward to spending time outdoors, you'll find the experience far more rewarding. Conversely, if you're susceptible to loneliness, tend to be impatient, or simply can't bear the thought of living without the conveniences and amenities of urban life, adjusting to rural life may prove difficult.

Obviously, whatever skills you possess will enhance your chances for success. If you have some farming experience or a green thumb, enjoy camping and hiking, and have a good grasp of carpentry, plumbing, engine repair or a background as an electrician, you'll probably be better equipped to face the challenge. This is not to say that you cannot adapt. Storey Publishing (Storey.com) offers a number of informative titles to readers interested in obtaining the practical skills and knowledge necessary for small-scale farming and homesteading. You can also investigate if there are any trade schools in your area that might allow you to expand your existing skills. If there are any nearby farms or community gardens, you might consider asking if you can help out on weekends so that you can gain some practical, hands-on experience.

It is also important that you enter this endeavor with a certain amount of pragmatism. While the hippie farmers of the '60s and '70s were strongly committed to living in accordance with their ideals, many of these experimental farms suffered crushing disappointments. Money was often a key issue. Many urban escapists believed that they could maintain a rural lifestyle with small sums of money, but these modest farming efforts were often labor-intensive and increasingly costly. Despite the best of intentions, crops sometimes failed, equipment broke down, financial pressures mounted and relationships began to fray. The small minority who thrived were primarily those who were able to maintain a steady source of income to supplement their agricultural earnings and afford much-needed supplies, repairs and renovations.

If money is a problem, you may need to move to a location that is close enough to a town or city where you can find work. Although the cost of living is less expensive in the country, if you plan on seeking employment, you probably won't earn as much as you would in a medium- or large-sized city. You may be required to hold down more than one job to make ends meet along with your daily chores. Fortunately, we live in the Internet Age, and there are economic opportunities available to consumers that may have made the difference for many '70s-era homesteaders.

One thing I've learned simply by staying alive this long is that even the most putridly corrupt economic system, even the biggest fraud of a government has an amazing resiliency. We may be dwelling in a house of cards, but it's as if the house is held together by bits of glue around its edges. It will fall. And it will be bad when it falls. But as to exact timing, I wouldn't want to guess. It *should* have fallen thirty years ago.

When the country goes into deep economic and social decline (and I still believe it's when, not if), it could be for many causes and take many forms. It could happen swiftly or (as it looks now) as a slow, dreary, continuing slide.

But as to what the country will look like "after," I think we doomsayers tend to overemphasize the extent of street-level social chaos that follows disaster (and I think that's true whether the disaster be economic collapse, food shortages, climate change or even a whole chain of such things). Will there be pockets of extreme violence? Sure. I wouldn't want to be living around people who've had a lifelong dependence on "entitlements" on the day the checks cease to arrive—or the checks arrive but will only buy half a loaf of bread. But I think that for the most part, history shows that no matter how bad things get, people cope.

Erich Maria Remarque, the German novelist who wrote *All Quiet on the Western Front*, also wrote a novel called *The Black Obelisk* about everyday life during the hyperinflation in Germany's Weimar Republic in the 1920s. He paints a vivid picture. People just went on with their daily lives, even when things got so bad that prices had to be recalculated several times a day. They just renegotiated, coped with the altered reality and went on living.

The biggest change was that they became cynical and gave up all their moral underpinnings in favor of a "live for today" attitude. And of course, in their disgust and desperation they also became perfect pawns for a man like Hitler, who offered them a villain they could blame for their troubles and promised them a better life.

Another example: Look at Zimbabwe today. 100,000 percent inflation. Eighty percent unemployment. Food shortages. Gas shortages. Total economic ruin beyond even some of the doomiest scenarios. But people there can't even rouse themselves to pitch Robert Mugabe and his cronies out of power. And even though Zimbabweans are in dire, dire straits, for the most part they don't riot or loot. They just cope. Not happily. But they cope.

Pursuing a home-based business or profession that doesn't require going into an office or business each day is a good way to ensure that money issues won't place limitations on where you choose to live. Learning new skills that are more in demand in the locality you have in mind is another possible option. However, for some people buying land may be out of the question, and leasing or renting a property may be the only option. If this is the case, some modern homesteaders recommend an incremental strategy. Start small, begin by renting, save your money and keep looking at properties. You might even consider pooling resources with friends or family so that you can share expenses and divide up the workload.

Country Life: Pros and Cons

IF YOU ARE DEAD SET ON LEAVING THE CITY OR SUBURBS, YOU MUST keep in mind that urban transplants sometimes have difficulty integrating themselves into small, rural communities. A well-founded suspicion of interlopers from out of the area can often create a barrier to friendly co-existence with your fellow residents—and this is not a minor matter. The survivalist scenario of setting up an isolated, country retreat stocked with food and fuel simply won't work. You will not be able to survive in the country without occasional assistance from your neighbors. Indeed, many modern homesteaders cite the joys of belonging to a small, close-knit community as one of the most positive facets of the homesteading experience. However, if you are friendly, open and polite, you shouldn't encounter many obstacles.

A vehicle with four-wheel drive is a must-have. Backcountry roads are often topped with gravel or dirt, and the few that are paved are sometimes filled with potholes. When the weather is wet, getting stuck in the mud is a common occurrence. Fuel costs will also be an additional burden. If you live far from the nearest town, it may take a quarter tank of gas just to fill up at the nearest service station. Getting sick or injured may also be a more trying experience. If you live in the sticks, you're not going to have the option of going to a nearby hospital with 24 hour urgent care, so a background in first aid or frontier medicine will go a long way. If you plan on raising livestock and growing crops, be prepared to toil each and every day, even if you're sick, tired or simply bored.

However, when you look beyond some of these minor drawbacks, there are innumerable benefits to rural living. For one thing, you probably won't miss the pollution. You'll get used to breathing clean air, drinking fresh water and seeing the stars each night without the hindrance of light pollution. There is also the psychological comfort of open space and endless vistas unhampered

Whatever happens five or ten or twenty years from now (and ultimately I don't expect it to be pretty), above all I believe that in their daily lives people will mostly plug along resignedly. They may make do with less, learn to barter, grow more of their own food, perhaps. They may die younger, beg on the streets more, live in extended-family households, and listen more avidly to demagogues and would-be saviors.

Millions will get a hard wake-up call when they learn that prosperity isn't their birthright and that government won't always rescue them from every danger. Some won't be able to handle that and will fall apart. But for others, it could even be a creative challenge leading to a greater ability to solve problems, stronger communities, more independence from large institutions.

But life will still be recognizably what it is today—barring some total catastrophe like an eruption of the Yellowstone supervolcano or an asteroid strike, which no one can predict; or barring, on the other hand, some fantastic technological advance that changes life for the better.

Either a major catastrophe or a major advance could happen. But if I were betting, I'd bet on something like normal life, just lived at a lower level.

Q: *What are you doing personally to address the anticipated outcome?*

CW: Well, I've written a lot… Waved my arms and shouted a lot of warnings. But aside from that…

Because I began my personal preparedness based on the doom scenario (what I now call the George Romero scenario, since a big part of the vision resembles a Hollywood zombie siege), a big part of my planning involved getting out into the country and far from main traffic and transportation routes. I've lived that way for the last thirty years and have come to enjoy this life for its own sake, regardless of what happens in the big world. It has helped me to develop something else that is hugely important (and underemphasized) in preparedness plans: an independent mindset.

You can have all the purchased preparations in the world, the coolest gear, the latest gadgets, the most expensive storage foods, the most expert manuals. But they won't avail you if you don't have a mindset for taking care of yourself and your own.

by buildings, billboards and smog. You will likely become healthier as you get used to eating fresh food and adjust to the calorie-burning daily exertions that will become a part of your daily routine. If you like gardening, hunting, camping, hiking, fishing and other outdoor activities, and if you find an ideal location, you can enjoy these pursuits to the fullest. If your cultivation efforts pay off, you can also look forward to a significantly reduced cost of living and the satisfaction of eating food that you've grown yourself.

There is also the welcome prospect of living without the underlying tensions of urban life, like crime, gridlock, overcrowding and pollution, and there is the freedom of being able to choose an entirely different way of living. If you've always dreamed of living off the grid, the country is a great place to experiment. If you live in a cramped apartment or small home, it's not exactly the best place to set up a compost toilet or gray water irrigation system. However, with ample open space, you can set up a wind turbine or photovoltaic solar panels to generate electricity, cook your meals with a solar cooker or Rocket Stove, or warm your home with an old-fashioned wood-burning stove.

Your Own Slice of Land

IF YOU'RE INTERESTED IN OPERATING YOUR OWN SELF-SUSTAINING farm, a good first step is contacting the Center for Rural Affairs (CFRA). The organization is a nationally known non-profit dedicated to building thriving rural communities, improving the environment and creating opportunities for small farmers and ranchers. The CFRA web page (cfra.org) has a section called the "Beginning Farmer and Rancher Opportunities Page" that provides information about locating available land, financing and guidance on how to market and sell your crops. CFRA also sponsors programs that offer loans, grants and technical training to small-scale farmers. There is even a "Land Link" section on the group's web page that will connect you with existing landowners who may own or lease a plot of land that might suit your needs.

If you're cash-strapped but determined to move to the country and you're not particular about where you settle, a few states are actually offering free land to boost rural populations and increase tax revenue. If you visit the Kansas Free Land web page (kansasfreeland.com), as of 2008 over a dozen cities are offering free plots of land and other incentives to modern-day settlers looking to relocate. The web page for the Nebraska Library Commission also offers a collection of links to cities offering incentive programs and possible land giveaways to individuals interested in homesteading (nebraskaccess.ne.gov/freeland.asp). However, some localities have specific requirements, such as

I also believe in all the typical things like storing food and water and investing in whatever hard assets you can afford—even if you can't afford much. And I've done what I can in that regard.

But my personal ability to own a lot of stuff has been compromised by a more fundamental choice I've made: to live simply. I've chosen to live in a one-room house, with few possessions and minimal income, but mostly debt free.

Simple living isn't for everybody and I'm not saying that it should be. But for me, a huge part of both daily life and preparation for future hard times involves just being independent. Nobody owns my future but me. No mortgage company. No vehicle finance company. No passel of credit-card vendors.

Some folks who expect high inflation say that incurring debt today can be good because you can pay it off cheaply tomorrow with less valuable dollars. Maybe so, but "living a debt life" is corrosive. It says, "Live for today and to hell with tomorrow." Worse, it says that the chase after stuff, stuff, stuff is more important than knowing ourselves and examining and living by more personal values.

I've got nothing against "stuff." If I had money, I'd surround myself with beautiful artworks, for instance. But stopping the eternal chase, getting off the "consumer" (hate that word) merry-go-round and getting centered in my own life has probably been the most important preparation for hard times that I've made. I know who I am. I know what I need. I know what matters to me and what I can, without undue sacrifice, let go of.

Still, I'd like to return to one aspect of conventional preparedness for a moment: food. Wendy McElroy has recently been pointing out that, with food inflation being what it is, buying canned foods and other storable foods *now* is actually a form of investment.

And of course, rotating stored foods and using them is important (even if time-consuming). I just heard a report on NPR that pointed out that before the first "instant" foods came along in the 1930s, an average American family spent up to four hours a day (of Mom's time) on food preparation. Now we spend that time watching TV and use only a half-hour a day, on average, fixing meals.

the construction of a home, before you can legally own the property, so you may incur some additional expenses.

Deals can also be found exploring properties on web pages like LandWatch. com and LandFlip.com. Both web pages have easy to use search applications that allow you to find and locate properties for lease or sale throughout the nation. If you'd like to purchase an existing farm, UnitedCountry.com has a similar search function that allows you to locate agricultural properties for sale within your individual price range. Before you consider purchasing a property that is under-priced or that is part of a free land program, you will need to remember that there may be a good reason: the region could be experiencing economic difficulties, drought or the soil could be poor quality. Be sure to look before you leap.

If your primary focus isn't farming, but finding an affordable place away from the cities with some available land to grow fruits and vegetables, homes are far more affordable in rural locations. Even if a home or farm is beyond your financial means, don't give up. Talk to the owner—he or she may be interested in setting up a lease-to-own or rental arrangement. If you've discovered a rural community that looks ideal for your individual needs, you can also take out advertisements in the local newspaper expressing what kind of place you are looking for and how much you'd be willing to spend. You have little to lose, and you might run across a great deal. Even if a property isn't up for sale, contacting the owner and making an offer has been known to pay off. At the very least, he or she may direct you to a nearby home or farm that is in your price range. If you have a background in carpentry or construction, you might locate a fixer-upper that can be purchased at a reduced price.

Before you decide to buy or rent a home or farm in the country, be sure to thoroughly investigate the property. Study what kind of rainfall and sunlight the region gets, average temperatures and other important data that could greatly impact your future cultivation efforts. There are also underlying legal issues that you should clarify with a local realtor, attorney or title company before moving in. Below are just a few important considerations that you should keep in mind:

Access: Do you have access to the road leading to your property or does this require your neighbor's consent?

Ownership: Is there an existing lien on the property? What are the exact boundaries of your property? Also remember that some farms can still be bound by dated (but valid) contracts that cede all rights to any

CLAIRE WOLFE continued

I've recently made a commitment to eating much more fresh food while also integrating my long-term storage foods, like wheatberries and dried legumes, into my regular diet. This takes a huge commitment of time. Grinding grains with a hand-grinder (practicing for a time when electricity might be scarce) is no fun at all, and takes forever. But the habit may come in handy someday. And in the near-term it pays off in better health.

Gardening and other forms of home food raising (bee keeping, goat-milk-ing, etc.) may also be increasingly important. I expect to see some pretty inter-esting urban, suburban and rural food production in the future.

But I admit that these are weak areas for me. They really aren't cost-effec-tive, and can be pretty expensive to get started with. Still, I grow a few things and help take care of the neighbors' chickens in exchange for eggs, and I think producing one's own food is an excellent idea for many reasons. This is some-thing I tell myself I ought to do more of.

I'm sure other people you talk with will emphasize firearms, shooting skills, homemade energy and so on, so I'll leave those topics alone. But I want to touch on one other thing I do that I believe is under-emphasized in the typi-cal "doom" scenario.

One of the most important things we can do is build a solid, trusted network of people—a circle of friends. We need people we can rely on and who can rely on us in moments of need. People we can trade with discreetly, people who'll watch our backs, people who have skills we may lack.

I feel very fortunate to have such circles in my own life, both in my local rural community and in a wider community of people I met first on the internet but later connected with in real life.

Q: *Do you believe Federal Reserve notes will continue to exist as the standard medium of exchange?*

CW: I truly hope not. The FRN has never been a benefit to us. I'd love to see it recognized as the worthless scrap scrip that it is.

Q: *I know that you don't want people to know where you live, but what brought you to this particular area?*

oil, natural, gas or minerals found on the property. While many of these outdated claims will lay dormant for decades, it's well worth your time to investigate—if your property is encumbered by any such agreements, there's a chance you might wake up one morning to the ear-splitting sound of heavy equipment.

Soil: Is the soil good quality? Are there any environmental issues surrounding your land or nearby properties?

Timber: If you plan on using a wood-burning stove, you will need a good supply of firewood, especially during the winter months. Are there any timber contracts on your property? Does your property allow you access to neighboring wooded areas or are these strictly off-limits? Is there an affordable source of firewood in the community?

Water Rights: Can you construct a well on your property? Is the region subject to droughts? Are there local water suppliers? Do you have access to use a nearby stream that borders your land parcel?

Waste Disposal: If you choose to install a septic system will you be in compliance with environmental regulations and local ordinances?

Zoning: Be sure to inquire about the land surrounding your property. It may be zoned for development that could adversely affect your quality of life. Can you raise livestock on your property? What sorts of buildings are allowed?

So what parts of the country are particularly conducive to a simpler, no-frills life? A few years back, *Mother Earth News* polled its readership for what they considered the best locations for the modern homesteader. The Pacific Northwest, with its moderate climes, clean air and nearby coast was at the top of the list. The numerous small towns that dot Oregon and Washington were highly recommended as ideal for resettling. A mixed economy, environmentally conscious locals and proximity to Canada only added to the allure. While a migratory surge of retirees, homesteaders and disaffected Californians has driven up land prices in this area, it's a picturesque part of the country that is well worth investigating.

The slice of country that encompasses northeast Indiana and parts of northwest Ohio was also given high marks, and described as the perfect

CW: I was drawn to this general area (the Pacific Northwest) for purely aesthetic reasons. I live in a place of great natural beauty. Heck, you can't do everything for practical, survival-oriented motives.

It also helps that this region is a Garden of Eden when it comes to natural food sources and water. Pacific Northwesterners may grow moss on their north sides from the crappy climate and may commit suicide in large numbers due to the perpetual gloom. But go thirsty? Not likely. Starve? Between the fishing, the foraging opportunities and the profligacy with which so many things grow here, it's hard to imagine. •

setting "If you like your land flat to gently rolling, supremely fertile and well-watered by slow, wide rivers with names like Flatrock and Maumee." The region possesses some of the nation's cheapest quality homes.[2] If you look beyond the noxious fumes emanating from the New Jersey turnpike, the "ecologically unique" southern part of the Garden State was also praised by readers as an idyllic location with a sizeable local economy and an excellent climate for small-scale farming. Further down the list were the less inhabited parts of Colorado, the entire state of Wisconsin, rural North Carolina and the swathe of land along the Appalachians that encompasses parts of Kentucky and West Virginia.

However, choosing where to live is truly a subjective decision. Everyone has their own particular needs and requirements. Above all else, be aware that you don't need hundreds of acres if your primary goal is subsistence farming. When the Soviet Union fell, many desperate Russian families were able to keep food on the table by maintaining a *sotka*—a 100-meter strip of land. If you'd like an excellent overview of how to grow your own food, Steve Solomon's *Gardening When It Counts: Growing Food in Hard Times* is highly recommended. Publications like *Mother Earth News* (motherearthnews.com) and *Backwoods Home* (backwoodshome.com) also provide a wealth of invaluable tips, guidance and information to would-be homesteaders.

Relocalization

LIVING IN THE COUNTRY ISN'T FOR EVERYONE. YOU MAY LACK THE resources or knowledge, or simply don't believe that you would be comfortable residing in a quiet, rural setting. Some of us are intensely social animals and require the crowded, electric atmosphere of a bustling city or town to truly feel alive. The leap from town to country is a major life-changing event, and you may be reluctant to make such a commitment. Additionally, the responsibilities inherent in operating a working homestead will require near-total dedication and a number of complex skills that can't be easily learned on the fly. Is there another way?

In recent years, a growing move toward relocalization is gaining traction as a possible response to system failures caused by an energy crisis, natural disasters or severe economic depression. Localization advocates, many who reside in urban areas, believe small, decentralized village-like communities that secure basic human needs (i.e., food, water, shelter and energy) on a local level will be more fuel efficient and less destructive to the environment.

Simplicity is the key. Everything will need to be done on a smaller scale, which will reduce the underlying complexities of modern society and make these sustainable communities more resilient than today's gridlocked megacities. Some relocalization scenarios even involve the creation of community currencies, the local production of key goods and services, and other measures designed to disconnect from the global financial system. Should a fuel shortage, economic upheaval or natural disaster impact the public's ability to secure basic needs, these small, independent communities will have the necessary resources to withstand these destabilizing events.

Beginning in 2003, the Post-Carbon Institute (postcarbon.org) has been providing guidance, resources and vital networking tools to the estimated 150 relocalization initiatives across the nation. The Post-Carbon Institute includes a directory on its web page of various post-carbon groups throughout the U.S. (relocalize.net). While many of these small-scale initiatives are still in the planning stages, others are moving toward implementation. If you're curious, be sure to find out if there are any relocalization groups in your area.

So what would life be like in a relocalized community? Perhaps the best way to describe these envisioned small-scale societies is to imagine a '60s-era hippie commune with a radical systems upgrade. Cutting-edge organic farming methods would be deployed to ensure the quality of food production. Community grids reliant on renewable energy sources like solar technology or wind power would be used to provide electricity. As these communities become more advanced, perhaps barter or community currency may be used instead of inflationary Federal Reserve notes. The first tentative steps toward the relocalization model can be seen in the growth of ecovillages.

The Ecovillage

ALTHOUGH THE FIRST SUCH VILLAGE WAS DEVELOPED IN RELATIVE obscurity in Davis, CA two decades ago, more environmentally-conscious, sustainable living arrangements are sprouting up with each passing year. As of 2008, there were at least one hundred communities in thirty-seven states—there were only sixty in 2006—and there are an estimated three hundred currently in the works.[3] There is no distinct cookie-cutter template for any given ecovillage. Each one seems to have its own unique flavor. There are upscale green housing complexes that utilize state-of-the-art "microgrid" technology and greenhouses. Some are rurally based and include acres of farmland. Others are geared toward providing affordable housing to low-income residents and creating a mixed community with people of all different income levels.

As consumers struggle with surging rental costs, burdensome mortgages and a sluggish economy, residing in a low-cost ecovillage could become a viable option. If you're interested in pursuing a serious lifestyle change that may help you cut costs and get you through the current economic difficulties, the Global Ecovillage Network (gen.ecovillage.org) provides an online directory that allows you to connect with self-sustaining communities in your area or in an outlying district.

Like living in the country, residing in a communal setting will likely be a matter of temperament. If you're not the social type, remember that you will be expected to take an active role in community life and may be asked to assist with group chores. However, many of these communities appear to be adequately prepared for any possible food or energy shortages, and individuals working together can often accomplish a great deal. If you're a gregarious, social type, and view the current economic situation as an opportunity to change your lifestyle and possibly head in a new direction, you might wish to consider joining an ecovillage as a possible retreat option.

Consider an Escape Hatch

BROADENING YOUR HORIZONS AND ADOPTING A NEW WAY OF LIFE needn't stop at the water's edge. It's a regrettable fact, but economic circumstances will sometimes send even the most dedicated patriot sprinting for the nearest exit. If you're one of the seven out of ten Americans who have never obtained a passport, you should reconsider. It's important to keep every option open, and this may include looking beyond America's borders for opportunities. You may never need it, but a passport guarantees your ability to travel freely, and it would be foolhardy to ignore the potential that may exist outside America's borders.

While the prospect of leaving the U.S. may sound unsettling, keep in mind that you won't be renouncing your citizenship or breaking your ties with America. You may just be biding your time until conditions change for the better. Once you've obtained a passport, take the time to research what country might be an amenable relocation option and how you would go about obtaining a visa and establishing residency. If you're unsure what would make for an attractive destination, Mark Ehrman's *Getting Out: Your Guide to Leaving America* is highly recommended. The book provides a comprehensive overview of expatriate living options throughout the world with valuable information on visa and residency requirements, employment and expert opinion on the best locations for visiting Americans. While your prospects abroad are somewhat beyond the scope of this work, let's briefly examine a couple of options.

Canada has long been a popular destination for Americans seeking a change. Nationalized health care, a primarily English-speaking population, access to the usual amenities and close proximity to the U.S. seem to make a perfect fit for many former Yanks. Unfortunately, settling in Canada isn't as easy as it sounds. There are six types of visas granted to prospective residents, and unless you have a relative living in Canada, you must show proof that you either possess a substantial net worth or some type of marketable skill that will contribute to the Canadian economy. If you'd like more information about how to obtain a Canadian visa, the government has set up a web page for immigrants (www.cic.gc.ca/ENGLISH/information/offices/index.asp).

If your finances are low and you don't have the adequate employment background, South or Central America may be your best bet. If your knowledge of Spanish is minimal, consider relocating to Mexico or Costa Rica. Both nations have sizeable expatriate communities and it won't be hard to find a few English-speaking locals to show you the ropes. If you have the time, learning Spanish will make your life a lot easier. Visas are relatively simple to obtain in either nation, and the cost of living is substantially lower than the U.S. Although jobs may be scarce, if you do some creative networking, you may be able to locate a paying position, a few leads or even an opportunity to start your own business. Obtaining land in a foreign country isn't easy, and the process can be complex, but if you're willing to commit yourself, land can be substantially cheaper, and homesteading in a foreign land might prove to be a worthwhile endeavor. There are ecovillages in South America as well.

Before you make a definite choice, be sure to explore web pages like EscapeArtist.com and ExpatExchange.com. Both sites offer resources, housing information, employment listings and guidance to the curious expatriate. While America's economic crisis may impact other parts of the world as well, you still might find a good location to wait out the recession, or possibly start a new life.

A Distant Future

WHETHER THE MOVE TOWARD MORE SUSTAINABLE LIVING AND adopting simpler lifestyles is an ephemeral trend or a radical departure remains to be seen. However, there is one definite certainty: the way that Americans have lived for the past few decades may be coming to an end. As Americans contend with Depression 2.0, we may need to harness our creative powers and radically overhaul how and where we choose to live. Weekend trips to the mall may give way to Sunday mornings at the farmer's market or grueling day hikes in the country. Who knows? Perhaps one day the dramatic shift in consciousness that characterized the 1970s Back to the Land movement will be remembered as the first tentative steps of a journey destined to culminate in the present age. •

Notes

1   Proulx, Annie. *What'll You Take for It?: Back to Barter*, (Garden Way: Vermont, 1981).

2   "The Ten Best Places to Live the Good Life," *Mother Earth News*, August/ September 1996.

3   Lizaire, Cassandra. "Communal Lifestyle Reborn," Columbia News Service, May 11, 2008.

CHAPTER 7

KEEPING THE LIGHTS ON
HOME ENERGY SOLUTIONS

Keeping the Lights on: Home Energy Solution

WHEN OIL SURGED PAST $100 A BARREL IN 2008, THE INHERENTLY fragile nature of our petroleum-based economy was brought into sharp relief. In just a few short months, the dollar sagged and inflation started climbing. Because U.S. agriculture is largely dependent on cheap fuel, food prices outpaced the Consumer Price Index for the first time in decades. Along with rising grocery costs, suburban commuters found their budgets thrown into disarray by exorbitant gas prices. Air travel, even for the shortest of trips, became prohibitively expensive. Many government services were hampered due to unexpected energy costs. In a few localities, precincts lowered gasoline costs by replacing traditional police cruisers with officers walking beats and even conducting bicycle patrols.

Whether you believe this was simply an aberration or the first ominous signs of what Peak Oil theorists call the "arc of depletion," as long as we remain dependent on imported oil, our lifestyles and incomes will hinge on the world's volatile petroleum markets. While the current economic crisis may be temporarily driving down consumer and public demand for oil, experts are warning that the brief reduction in oil prices may not last for long, and we could find ourselves contending with another steep rise in energy costs as increasing demand starts to erode existing reserves. "In terms of non-OPEC countries," remarked Fatih Birol, Chief Economist of the International Energy Agency, in a December 2008 interview, "we are expecting that in three, four years' time, the production of conventional oil will come to a plateau, and start to decline."[1]

U.S. consumers will likely be the first to bear the brunt of any future energy shortfalls or price hikes. In the summer of 2008, when oil prices were at record highs, *USA Today* reported that utility companies throughout the nation were "disconnecting more consumers who fall behind on their bills" and that even "moderate-income households" were "getting zapped."[2] According to the article, the number of customers in 2008 who had either their natural gas or electricity turned off due to non-payment of bills spiked by an estimated 15% in a number of states. In Detroit—where unemployment is high and brutally cold winters are the norm—the number of natural gas shutoffs rose by an estimated 50%.

In light of the current energy situation, consumers may find that maintaining sufficient electricity could become a constant struggle in the near future. It is worth keeping in mind that oil isn't the only precious commodity running in short supply. A sizeable number of power plants in the U.S. run on coal and natural gas. Unfortunately, the nation's diminishing natural gas reserves and a growing shortage of high-quality coal will make it difficult to meet public demand for electricity, which is expected to surge by over 25% in the next two decades.[3] We must also remember that our day-to-day power use will likely be affected by the long neglect of our nation's power grid, and we could start witnessing more and more blackouts. Indeed, the ability to cope with a major power loss and move toward energy self-sufficiency will be a valuable asset to have in the years ahead.

Aging Grid, Rising Costs

THE NATION'S SPRAWLING POWER SYSTEM IS COMPRISED OF THREE regional grids connected by an estimated 160,000 miles of high-voltage transmission lines. The network of power lines direct energy to state and local substations where the high-voltage electricity is "stepped down" to a lower-voltage current and then distributed to American households. The key concept is interconnectivity. These "grid linkages," as they are called, add resilience to the system by allowing a utility company in one area to make up any possible shortfalls by drawing electricity generated in another area.

Unfortunately, the system's greatest strength is also its Achilles' heel. When something goes wrong, this underlying interdependence can trigger a paralyzing chain reaction, like in 2003, when a series of power lines in Northern Ohio went down due to an inopportune collision with overhanging branches, and set off the historic Northeast Blackout. Experts believe that outdated equipment was also partly to blame for the record-setting power outage. Until the national power grid is radically overhauled, the system will remain vulnerable to disruptions and system failures.

There's also a good chance that your local utility company is plagued by some of the same problems we are seeing on a national level due to decades of negligence and underinvestment. In just a few short years, there have been power outages in large major cities like Detroit, Chicago and Houston. In one of the worst incidents, residents of Queens, New York suffered a blackout in summer 2006 that left thousands without access to electricity during the hottest days of the year. The power loss was attributed to the failure of twenty-two aged high-voltage feeder cables. Seven excruciating days would go by before

Con Edison was able to start restoring electricity to most of the area's beleaguered residents. The more unfortunate would wait even longer.

Perhaps it is time to start making contingency plans. Necessity, as the saying goes, is all too often the mother of invention. The longer that critical infrastructure needs go ignored by unresponsive government institutions, and the more expensive that energy becomes, the more likely we will see resourceful and innovative citizens working toward developing alternative home energy systems or decentralized community power grids that will allow for greater flexibility and preparedness.

Sizing Up Your Power Needs

AT SOME POINT, WE'VE ALL EXPERIENCED A BLACKOUT. IN MOST instances, it's merely a minor inconvenience. We grab a flashlight or lantern, maybe light a few candles and peer out the window into the ominous darkness. Usually within a few hours, or by the next day, the lights are back on, the comforting hum of the refrigerator has returned, and everything is back to normal.

We provided a few general strategies for coping with blackouts in a previous chapter. However, the 2006 blackout in Queens, New York was far from a momentary outage. Consider how you would cope if forced to go seven days without electricity. Keep in mind, most blackouts tend to occur when energy use peaks, which is typically on either the hottest or coldest days of the year. For some people, going without critical electricity needs may not be an option. This is when some type of backup power can be a real lifesaver.

Before we discuss emergency power options, the first important step is assessing your energy requirements. When making your calculations, try to be conservative and stick to the basics: lighting, heating and cooling, computers and possibly a security system should form the core of your emergency power needs. Some appliances you may view as "must-haves," like dishwashing machines or coffee makers. However, these items are closer to luxuries, and you should consider doing without them if you can. Once you've put together a basic list of your most valued appliances, you will need to calculate your total wattage requirements.

The web page for Consumer Reports (consumerreports.org), a non-profit publication devoted to product safety and consumer awareness, offers a helpful, easy to use home wattage calculator that should simplify the process. What's great about this program is that once you've checked off all of your appliances, the online application will recommend what type of home generator will best address your energy needs. If you'd like to make a rough estimate, consult the list below.

Appliance	Wattage
A/C (Central)	5,000
A/C (Room)	1,000
Alarm Clock	10
Central Heating (gas furnace)	400
Central Heating (oil furnace)	1,500
Coffee Maker	1,050
Computer (desktop w/ monitor)	125
Computer (laptop)	25
DVD Player	25
Fan (ceiling)	120
Fan (window)	150
Heating (electric)	1,125
Lighting (incandescent)	100
Lighting (compact fluorescent)	25
Microwave Oven	925
Stove (electric)	4,500
Refrigerator	725
Television (26-inch LCD)	110
Television (36- to 42-inch Plasma)	340
Toaster Oven	1,225
Water Heater	5,000

Source: *Consumer Reports* (consumerreports.org)

If you're unsure what the requirements are for a given appliance, voltage and wattage information can be found on the product's identification plate next to the model and serial numbers, or in the owner's manual. If the requirements are listed in amps instead of watts, remember that watts are calculated by multiplying amps by voltage. For instance, if you have an appliance that runs on ten volts and requires 200 amps, the required wattage will be 2,000. Remember that some appliances that are motor-driven, like refrigerators, often require more than double the wattage for the first second or two during startup. This spike is called the inductive load and can be a significant drain on electricity. For example, an older model refrigerator may only require

1,200 watts to operate in normal conditions, but may need 3,000 watts when the unit first powers up. Bear this in mind.

Once you've arrived at your estimated energy load, try paring it down to a more manageable level. This is where you'll need to be creative. Cooking all your meals in the microwave or using an outdoor stove may be inconvenient, but you won't have to deal with the heavy power drain of operating an electric stove. You may want to forego the coffee maker for a few days and heat your warm beverages in the microwave. Try using fans instead of A/C when possible. Keeping a small refrigerator on hand for emergencies will significantly cut down your energy requirements. Warming yourself by the fireplace or using a space heater may be preferable to powering up the energy-guzzling furnace. The more you scale back your power requirements, the more options you will have.

Home Generators

IF YOU'RE A HOMEOWNER, NOT OPPOSED TO BURNING FOSSIL FUELS, and are dead set on enjoying all the amenities of civilization during a sustained blackout, look no further than a gasoline-powered generator. Although once notorious for emitting an ear-splitting racket, today's models are more fuel-efficient and less hazardous to the ears. Depending on your power needs, companies like Coleman, Honda and Kohler make a variety of units capable of providing between 2,200 and 7,000 watts for days on end. For a reliable, low-noise unit, be prepared to spend somewhere between $1,000 and $3,000.

However, there are several drawbacks to gasoline-powered generators that you must also keep in mind. For one, if your power is out for several days, you could be looking at a costly fuel bill, as most gas-powered models require several gallons per day to power a modern household. You must also remember that most service station gasoline pumps are powered by electricity so you may not have the option of replenishing your gas supply during a power outage.

If you plan on storing surplus fuel, you will need to find a safe, well-ventilated shed or storage area that is as far away from your home as you can manage and won't be near any sources of heat or ignition sparks that may cause a fire. Because the key chemicals in gasoline tend to break down or evaporate, you will also need to either rotate your fuel on a regular basis or add a fuel stabilizer. Be warned: even the smallest gas-powered unit will produce deadly carbon monoxide, so you will need to make sure you operate your generator in a location that has adequate ventilation. Never, under any circumstances, operate a gasoline-powered generator inside your home.

Because of these many drawbacks, some prefer natural gas as a fuel source. Although these units are somewhat more expensive, there are natural gas-powered stationary (or standby) generators that can be connected directly to your gas line, which will provide immediate backup power during a blackout. When the power fails, an automatic transfer switch will shut down utility wires and safely hook up the generator feed. These units will also continue to monitor your utilities and seamlessly shut the system down when the blackout is over, reconnecting you to the main power grid. Kohler's 12RESL runs close to $4,000 but produces over 10,000 watts, and is considered one of the better standby models on the market. Keep in mind that installing a stationary generator will run an additional $500-1,000, and having an electrician set up a transfer switch usually costs between $500–750.

Kohler and other manufacturers also make both portable and stationary models that use propane (also called liquefied petroleum gas or LPG). Although costlier than gasoline, LPG is considered both safer and cleaner, and it has an indefinite shelf life. When stored in large 250-gallon tanks, propane can provide power for several days. However, if you plan on using a propane-powered generator, you may need to obtain a permit, and some localities may not allow its use.

If you decide to purchase a home generator, there are a few important considerations to keep in mind:

Do it Right: Before purchasing a standby generator, remember that most localities require permits that you will need to acquire. You should also take the time to discuss the matter with your local utility company. They may have safety concerns or important guidelines that you will need to follow. Consult with a qualified electrician if you have any questions about installation, use, maintenance or safety concerns.

Transfer Switching: If you've installed a standby generator, be aware that you run the risk of your emergency power backfeeding to local power lines and possibly electrocuting utility company employees who may be working on downed lines during a blackout. There is also the risk that the power may be restored and that you and your home could be endangered by an enhanced electricity load. Make sure you have a transfer switch installed, and be sure to contact your local utility provider for more information about possible safety issues that may arise.

Upkeep: Most generators require constant upkeep and should be run periodically to make sure that everything is in working order. Consult your owner's manual for information about general maintenance. If your generator is in need of repair, don't wait for a blackout to find out.

Connections: Never, under any circumstances, plug your generator directly into a wall outlet. Use extension cords to connect appliances to your generator.

Fuel Safety: As we mentioned, store all gasoline or fuel in a safe, well-ventilated location that is free from heat or possible sparks that may cause a fire. Never run your generator inside your home. When running your unit outdoors, make sure the exhaust fumes aren't seeping into windows and doors, as you could suffer carbon monoxide poisoning. Never refuel your generator while the unit is running. Make sure that you store gasoline in American National Standards Institute (ANSI)-approved containers.

Lighten Your Load: If you plan on running an emergency generator, try to limit your overall power use by purchasing fuel-efficient, Energy Star-qualified appliances (energystar.org). This will reduce your power load, and you will burn less fuel. When in use, try to limit your power usage to the bare minimum. If you overload the generator it can be permanently damaged and can be a fire hazard as well.

Battery Power

IF YOU LIVE IN AN APARTMENT, YOUR OPTIONS WILL BE LIMITED IN terms of emergency power. Most high-wattage gasoline-powered generators cannot be safely operated in an apartment setting due to the dangers of fire and the threat of carbon monoxide poisoning. However, some buildings have standby generators, so you may want to investigate this subject with your landlord. Perhaps if you and some of your fellow tenants agree to chip in for the cost of a natural gas or propane-powered standby unit, he or she may be amenable to installing some type of emergency power source.

If you're a renter who requires some type of backup power, or you own a home but a generator simply isn't feasible, then at the very least you can set up an interim power arrangement that will allow you to enjoy some indoor lightning, cook your meals and run a few rudimentary electrical appliances. Before you start examining your emergency power options, it might be a good idea to adopt some of the energy-saving measures in Chapter 5. The more you limit your household energy use, the easier it will be to transition to grid-free power generation.

One possible option is running an inverter. Inverters convert direct current (DC) energy from the power grid that can be stored in a backup battery. Then, should the power go out, the inverter would convert the DC power in the battery into alternating current (AC), which can then be used in your home. The more basic models can be hooked directly to your car battery, but you must keep in mind that this might not be the best fit for home electricity needs.

Most automobile batteries on the market are geared toward providing a significant amount of current over a short period of time. This burst of energy allows the motor to turn over when you start your car. Once the engine has started, the alternator takes over and the battery goes back to charging. This explains why most car batteries can last several years. Because of the specific function of most car batteries, most models on the market don't have a great deal of reserve capacity, and can easily run down. Moreover, this setup may prove cumbersome over time, as you will need to continually run your engine to make sure your battery is sufficiently charged.

For a slow, steady current that won't quickly drain the battery and will help you keep your household running during a blackout, your best bet are deep-cycle batteries like the kind used in recreational vehicles and boats. Trojan Battery Company (trojan-battery.com) offers a variety of six, eight and twelve-volt batteries that are relatively affordable and are designed for durability and repeated charges. If you buy more than one, the batteries can be banked together for increased wattage. If you'd like to save a few dollars, consider purchasing Trojan's six-volt golf cart batteries, which run for about $100 apiece and are great for home power applications.

If you plan on running multiple batteries, it may be a good idea to purchase two inverters: one for small-voltage items like your laptop or cellular phone and one for larger appliances. The higher wattage inverters can inadvertently damage your more delicate low-power electronic items. Remember to be very careful with your batteries. The vapors they produce can be flammable, so make sure you keep them in a well-ventilated area. Maintenance is also crucial, and primarily involves adding distilled (don't use tap!) water to ensure that the lead plating is properly immersed in the chemical solution. If you neglect to do this, your batteries could become a serious fire hazard. If you're interested in a safer alternative, Sundance Solar (sundancesolar.com) makes a twelve-volt absorbed glass mat (AGM) battery for about $30 more that is safe, leak-proof and requires no maintenance.

Photovoltaic Solar

IF YOU HAVE AN INVERTER AND A SET OF BATTERIES, AND YOU'RE thinking of making the transition to greater energy independence, investing in photovoltaic (PV) solar panels might be your next logical step. PV panels produce energy by trapping the light produced by the sun, which is then converted into electricity. Each panel is comprised of solar cells that are linked together into modules. Each individual cell is made up semi-conductors, which are primarily made of silicon. When sunlight strikes the panels, they absorb the energy and produce a form of DC electricity that your inverter can convert into AC for household use. However, before you make the leap you will need to keep in mind that solar energy is still an evolving technology. In some instances, the process of converting the solar-generated DC electricity into AC will result in a loss of some of the energy your panels generated from the sun.

When setting up your panels, make sure you place them either on your roof or in an area that will get uninterrupted sunlight. If the sun is obstructed in any way, your solar panels will produce significantly less energy. You will also need a charge controller, which will alert you when your batteries require charging and help you avoid overcharging. In most urban locales you will be required to install a safety disconnect so that you can properly maintain your solar setup without risk of electrocution.

Along with the intrinsic benefits of living a more environmentally conscious lifestyle, allocating a greater portion of your energy requirements to a solar system will make you that much more resilient to fluctuating energy costs and possible disruptions to the national power grid. Low Impact Living (lowimpactliving.com), a web page dedicated to off-grid living, reports that the average cost of household solar systems has dropped by an estimated 80%, and as the market grows and manufacturing methods become more streamlined, competition may drive down prices even further.

To provide incentive, at least ten states offer cash and tax breaks to lure consumers away from the overburdened power grid. Indeed, utility companies in many U.S. states are so desperate to reduce power use that they will provide subsidies to those willing to make the switch to alternative energy. It might be a good idea to check with your local utility company or state governor's office to see if there are any programs in your area that provide financial assistance to people seeking energy independence. You can also check the Database of

State Incentives for Renewables and Efficiency (dsireusa.org). There are also federal tax credits available to people who invest in solar heating systems. Check out (energystar.gov) for more information.

If you can't afford the expense of a large-sized PV solar system, you can still use existing solar technology to provide basic emergency power for smaller household electrical appliances. The aforementioned Sundance Solar makes a variety of easy to use solar starter kits that include maintenance-free AGM batteries, solar panels, mounting brackets, inverters, charge controllers and all the additional accessories you will need to set up a basic system. Depending on your budget, you can rely on solar energy to power everything from your iPod to your television, and smaller appliances if you'd like a bit more power. The kits cost a few hundred dollars, but this might be a good initial investment if you're curious about alternative power and would like to experiment.

Off-Grid Cooking

IF YOU'D PREFER SOMETHING A LITTLE MORE BASIC, SOLAR COOKERS are a creative way to utilize the sun's energy to cook your meals. To make a crude solar oven, all you need is a dark colored pot, some cardboard and some aluminum foil. Glue the aluminum foil onto the cardboard, shiny side up. When gluing the foil, it's important that you avoid wrinkles, as this can impede the sun's reflected light and will make cooking harder. Make sure that you use a sizeable piece of cardboard, as you will need to bend the material in place so that it surrounds the pot and so the tinfoil side is pointed directly at the sun. If you place your pot in an oven-cooking plastic bag, it will retain even more heat, and increase in efficiency. Make sure your oven is off the ground, as contact with the earth or floor can result in a loss of heat. You will also need to adjust your cooker periodically to follow the movements of the sun.

Solar cooking requires adequate sunlight and takes a great deal longer to heat your meals than a conventional oven, but it's still a good option to have at your fingertips in the event of a power outage. In an emergency, you can also use the cooker to boil or disinfect water. If you'd prefer something a bit more elaborate, there are also box cookers and parabolic solar ovens that are far more efficient. SolarCooking.org is an invaluable web resource for solar cooking information.

Perhaps the most groundbreaking recent innovation in off-grid cooking is the Rocket Stove, created by Dr. Larry Winiarski of the Aprovecho Research Center. Introduced in the late 1990s, this amazing oven allows you to cook a meal using only a handful of twigs, branches, paper or scraps of wood as fuel. The stoves are more than just economical and fuel-efficient—these

DIY cookers also release far fewer pollutants than a traditional cooking fire. Moreover, the simple design allows for versatility and any number of improvements and variations.

If you'd like to construct your own, you will need a five-gallon metal container, a stove pipe, a stove pipe elbow, a 15-ounce can, a small metal grill and some type of material for insulation like ashes or sand.

- Begin by cutting a four-inch hole on the side of your metal container, a couple inches from the bottom. This is the opening where you will place your stove pipe elbow and feed your fire.
- You will need to ensure that air can pass freely underneath your kindling, so you must build a shelf that fits snugly into the center of your elbow opening. Using a can opener, remove both ends of your can and, using tin snips, cut the can lengthwise and unroll it so it takes on a flat, rectangular shape. Trim the metal into a "T"-shape that allows the narrow end to fit into your elbow and the wider end to protrude outward.
- Using your tin snips, cut a four-inch hole in the center of your container lid. Make sure your hole fits tightly over your stovepipe. Trim the edges off of the lid so it can be placed a few inches lower inside the container and directly over your insulating material.
- Measure and trim your stovepipe so that it will rest approximately an inch below the top of your container. Attach the stovepipe to your elbow and insert the fuel shelf into the mouth of the elbow.
- Once you have everything assembled, before putting your lid on, add insulation by packing wood ash or sand alongside the stovepipe inside your container. This will lock in heat.
- Place your grill on top of the container, and you're ready to cook!

To start your fire, insert some scrap paper or dry tinder underneath the fuel shelf and light. You will then insert your fuel (twigs, wood scrap, branches, etc.) into the elbow opening. Sometimes it helps to blow on the fire. Once your fire has started, place your pot directly over the fire and simply push your kindling inside the oven as the fire burns. Be warned! Rocket Stoves can reach temperatures in excess of 600 degrees, so be sure to operate your stove in a safe outdoor area, and exercise caution when using.

If you'd like a bit more detailed instruction, or are interested in possible design variations, there are a number of instructional videos and downloadable plans on the internet. The web page for the Aprovecho Research Center is a good place to start (aprovecho.org), and RocketStoves.org offers publications and videos for consumers interested in Rocket Stoves.

Cooling and Heating

WHILE IT'S ONE THING TO CELEBRATE OFF-GRID LIVING FROM THE MILD climate of Northern California, to someone facing a bone-chilling Michigan winter or the dog days of an Arizona summer, the prospect of losing power can have serious implications. If you'd like to make your home or apartment a bit more habitable when the cold or warm weather season arrives, take the time to make sure your place is properly insulated. Most homes and apartments are usually too cold or warm due to the presence of air leaks that expose the building to the elements. This helps explain why nearly half of all household energy use goes toward either raising or lowering the atmospheric temperature.

Experiencing a blackout in the middle of a heavy cold snap can result in severe discomfort and possibly hypothermia in regions known for harsh winters. If you haven't taken the time to caulk and seal all air leaks, you'll wish you had should a heavy storm come your way. If you'd like to further reduce heat loss, you can place thermal curtains in front of windows using plastic sheets, blankets, bubble wrap or even carpeting. If you have an attic or crawlspace, a few extra layers of insulation will also keep heat from escaping. If you only have limited emergency power, and you don't have the wattage to run your furnace or a space heater, consider constructing a larger Rocket Stove capable of heating your home. *Rocket Mass Heaters: Superefficient Woodstoves You Can Build* by Ianto Evans and Leslie Jackson provides step-by-step instructions for deploying Rocket Stove technology for home heating.

Proper insulation and sealing will also go a long way toward keeping you from burning up during the worst days of summer. A container garden can also help keep your residence cooler during summer. Consider setting up some water-hungry plants adjacent to your home or apartment windows to bring the temperature down. If you own your home, a solar-powered attic van can significantly lower both your energy costs and keep your home cool should the power go out. Sunrise Solar offers models that cost over $600, but the units are capable of monitoring attic temperatures, and will activate when the thermostat goes above eighty degrees and then shut down once the air has cooled.

The Way Forward

WHILE THE SHEER NUMBER OF EMERGING GREEN TECHNOLOGIES IS a bit beyond the scope of this book, the growth and popularity of solar, wind-powered and other alternative energy options is a welcome development that will make consumers that much more resilient in the future. According to a May 25, 2008 Reuters article, an estimated 350,000 Americans have already unplugged from the national power grid, and as the technology becomes more affordable and advanced, this number is predicted to run into the millions. While running a household using alternative energy once required a life of monk-like austerity, contemporary off-grid living now includes all the comforts of home. "You can have hot showers and a cold beer," Lonnie Gamble, an off-grid enthusiast, explained to Reuters. "You have no water bill, no sewer bill and you can harvest something fresh from the greenhouse... why would you ever do anything else?"[4]

Whatever strategy you choose to see you through any future power failures, at the very least try to formulate a basic plan that will lessen your reliance on the power grid and start taking the first tentative steps toward energy independence. If you can afford the added expense, alternative energy systems are a surefire way to stay connected during difficult economic times, build greater community preparedness and perhaps help ensure the future of the planet. •

Notes

1   Monbiot, George. "When Will the Oil Run Out?," *The Independent*, December 15, 2008.

2   Davidson, Paul. "Utilities Cut Off More Customers Who Are Behind on Their Bills," *USA Today*, June 23, 2008.

3   English, Glenn. "Rising Cost of Power, Plus Growing Demand, Could Lead to Blackouts," *Modesto Bee*, July 15, 2008.

4   Gaynor, Tim. "Pioneers Show Americans How to Live 'Off-Grid,'" Reuters, May 25, 2008.

CHAPTER 8

BETWEEN THE CRACKS
WHEN YOU HAVE NO SHELTER

Between the Cracks:
When You Have No Shelter

IT'S NOT THE MOST COMFORTING THOUGHT IN THE WORLD, BUT HERE in the U.S., economic crises and homelessness often go hand in hand. Over a century ago, when the panic of 1893 paralyzed the nation's economy, thousands of unemployed laborers joined what Gilded Age journalists called the "Army of the Unemployed," and took to the road in search of a fresh start or simply to ride out the economic hard times. It was a harsh and dangerous existence that revolved around hopping freights, artfully cadging meals, sleeping outdoors in primitive hobo jungles and staying one step ahead of local vagrancy laws and club-wielding railroad police. A generation later, the Great Depression set off another exodus, as hundreds of thousands of men, women and children took up the tramping life in a desperate search for work and a possible new beginning. Others stayed behind and found refuge in the thousands of crude shantytowns ("Hoovervilles") and primitive shelters that became a common sight during the Great Depression.

While we'd like to think we live in a more enlightened age, it's difficult not to detect an unsettling sense of déjà vu. Although most of America's large cities—like Chicago, Los Angeles, New York and Atlanta—have made inroads at reducing homelessness, the epic financial meltdown may reverse this trend and possibly add to the ranks of Americans without adequate shelter. As the foreclosure epidemic takes its toll, untold numbers of families and individuals are finding themselves displaced, without sufficient resources to transition to an apartment or home. Long before the current crisis ever materialized, advocates for the homeless were sounding the alarm that shelters and social service agencies were witnessing a sudden surge in new applicants. "Shelters are full and it's getting worse," Michael Stoops of the National Coalition for the Homeless informed *USA Today* in June 2008.[1] Commentators are calling this ominous trend the "new face" of homelessness.

This could be you. The path to homelessness is rarely the epic tragedy we often envision. Sometimes it's simply a string of unavoidable mishaps or just plain bad luck. You might gamble on finding work in a new town or city and strike out, leaving yourself without enough money to pay rent. A serious injury, a layoff or a financial emergency could drain your savings and leave you destitute and unable to pay your bills. Perhaps your landlord has fallen behind on his mortgage payments and you may be forced to move out of your affordable apartment. When your resources are limited, dealing with an eviction notice isn't any less traumatic than a foreclosure.

If you find yourself in a difficult situation where time is running out, and you can't locate suitable shelter, you will likely feel an overwhelming sense of fear, rage and desperation. This is a perfectly human response to an understandably frightening situation. However, you cannot allow these emotions to cloud your thinking. You will be making critical decisions, so you must remember to keep a cool head. Take a deep breath, and remind yourself that your problems are likely only temporary, and that you will find a solution.

Public Assistance

IF YOU ARE DESTITUTE AND HOMELESS, THE DECISION OF WHETHER or not to apply for public aid is a philosophical question best left up to the reader. Whatever your choice, there are a few positives and negatives to keep in mind. On the positive side, a small monthly injection of cash and food stamps may significantly lighten your load and keep you from going hungry. Additionally, most welfare programs provide free health care to the indigent, so at the very least you can look forward to cost-free medical care if you should become sick or injured. The growing popularity of "welfare-to-work" programs means that you may also receive some form of job placement or employment referrals as part of your benefit package, which may lead to a much-needed survival job while you get back on your feet. If you don't come from a state with a large population, you may also be referred to low-income subsidized housing if there are apartments available.

Unfortunately, as anyone who has been down on his luck will attest, the process of obtaining financial or material assistance through a typical state or municipal bureaucracy can be laborious and time-consuming. You may find yourself filling out endless reams of paper work and spending hours waiting in interminable lines to file the various forms and declarations required to fulfill eligibility requirements. There will be little margin for error; even the smallest mistake or oversight can delay your badly needed assistance checks. You will then be forced to repeat the entire tedious process all over again. The greater your desperation, the more likely the system won't be able to provide assistance in a timely manner. If you're a stickler for privacy, you must also remember that every shred of information about your economic life (savings, bank accounts, earnings, employment history) will need to be disclosed. You may even find yourself turning down work lest you earn too much and have your benefits taken away.

Whatever your decision, keep in mind that you have every right to apply for assistance. At the very least, it's probably a good idea to investigate how to obtain benefits in your area. If you're curious about what's available and how the process works, the Department of Health and Human Services (HHS) maintains a state-by-state listing of social service providers (www.hhs.gov/faq/families/1965.html). If you plan on applying, remember that you will need to have a valid form of identification, Social Security card, recent bank statements and tax records, and any other information that may be pertinent to your financial status. On a more sobering note, you will also need to bear in mind that an intractable recession could seriously impact a great many social programs due to the scarcity of tax dollars and the likelihood that a greater number of people will be applying for public assistance. The money simply may not be there.

Homelessness Must-Haves

BEFORE YOU HIT THE STREETS, MAKE SURE THAT YOU HAVE EXPLORED every available option. If you can't afford to rent an apartment, scour community bulletin boards and the internet and see if you can't locate a low-cost roommate situation or possibly rent someone's spare bedroom, den or garage. If you've cultivated a strong social network, now is the time to start doing some outreach and asking for assistance. Always remember, false pride won't keep you dry and warm on a cold rainy night. If you have to spend a few weeks or months sleeping on the couch of a friend, associate, relative or even an ex-spouse, this would be far preferable to living on the streets. Additionally, a stable home life will help you get back on your feet that much sooner. However, if you've exhausted every available alternative and you still haven't found any sort of suitable shelter, there are a few important arrangements you will need that you can't afford to ignore.

Storing your valuables and belongings should be your first order of business. Since you won't be making mortgage payments or paying rent, you may want to consider leasing a storage unit. Depending on where you live, prices usually run from between $30–50 per month for a smaller 5' x 5' unit to $200–400 for the larger 10' x 30' units. If you're strapped for cash, you may have a friend or relative who will let you use his or her home, apartment or garage to temporarily store your possessions. If you aren't sure, now is the time to ask, as cost-free storage will greatly reduce your overhead and allow for increased mobility.

Your social network should prove helpful in passing along housing leads and other helpful information that you might find useful. Therefore, it will be vital that you maintain your electronic ties with close friends and associates. A great many public libraries provide free internet access, so be sure you have a webmail account with Yahoo, Gmail or Hotmail that can be accessed from remote locations. If you can, try to keep up payments to your cell phone provider as well. If not, convenience stores like Wal-Mart offer inexpensive prepaid cellular phones that don't require a billing address and usually come with up to one hundred minutes of phone time. You can add refill minutes by going to PrePaidOnline.com.

However, if you can't afford a basic cellular phone, many localities have what is called community voice mail (CVM). CVM is a free, personalized, twenty-four-hour voice mail offered to indigent residents. If you are interested, the CVM web page (cvm.org) maintains a list of providers in the U.S. You may also wish to send or receive traditional mail. Ask a friend, relative or social service agency if you can use their mailing address. If not, consider opening up a post office box or setting up a mail service. This may be an added expense, but if you plan on applying for public assistance or doing any sort of correspondence you will need a dependable mailing address.

On the Streets

IF YOU DON'T OWN A VEHICLE, LIVING WITHOUT SHELTER WILL BE particularly challenging. You won't have the mobility and built-in shelter that a car can provide, but these obstacles aren't insurmountable. Be sure to make the necessary arrangements we recommended in the previous section for storage, e-mail, cell phone, etc. If you live in a part of the country where it can be bitterly cold, consider relocating. If you can afford the added expense, take a Greyhound or Amtrak to a warmer locale. If you decide to stay in a cold-weather climate with limited housing options, you will be running the very serious risk of being caught outdoors in the bitter cold and possibly placing your life in jeopardy.

Your first instinct might be to connect with a nearby homeless shelter. Unfortunately, you must keep in mind that many who have experienced homelessness strongly advise against staying in publicly-run shelters, especially in highly populated urban areas. Many of these institutions are understaffed, crowded, claustrophobic and often downright filthy. Some of your fellow residents will be hardened ex-convicts, and because there is often minimal security, theft and violence are not uncommon. This is not to say that there aren't exceptions to this rule. There are some privately-run shelters that offer a safe, clean environment for people to clean up and get warm, so be sure to investigate what homeless shelters serve your area, and you may find a few that offer something more than an institutional, prison-like experience. If you're not sure where to begin, Homeless.com is a good starting point, as is Artists Helping Children, which maintains an online directory of shelters across the U.S. (artistshelpingchildren.org).

Why not provide your own shelter? Purchasing a sturdy backpack like the kind used by backpackers, and a collapsible tent, will allow you greater mobility and independence. Depending on what items you plan on carrying, you will want a pack with somewhere between 3,500 and 5,800 cubic inches of capacity. As far as tents go, make sure that you buy one that is lightweight, well constructed and easy to set up, especially if you don't have much camping experience. Apache Instant Tents are a good choice (apachetents.com), as they are both lightweight and easy to pitch. Along with your tent, the following items should come in handy:

- Sleeping bag and pillow (bag liner if you are in a colder climate)
- Sleeping pad or ground sheet
- Blankets
- Plastic tarp for insulation and general use
- Spare clothing (including rain poncho, extra shoes and socks)
- Food (seven-day supply, seal in plastic bags, double bag to avoid leakage)
- Mess kit
- Water
- Items for personal hygiene (use a plastic or nylon bag)
- Baby wipes and liquid soap for emergency situations
- Paper towels
- First aid kit

- Flashlight or lantern (hand-crank or solar-powered may be a good choice)
- Portable radio (crank or solar-powered)
- Plastic bags (for possible waste disposal) and toilet paper
- Duct tape and cord
- Swiss Army knife, can opener and other basic tools
- Mace, pepper spray or other weapon for self-defense

As a general rule, you may want to avoid areas where numerous homeless people congregate, such as freeway underpasses, outside welfare offices, business districts, etc. Sadly, some people get their thrills preying on people they perceive as weak, and many homeless people are victims of senseless and brutal attacks. You must also keep in mind that the homeless community that exists in your town will likely be a microcosm of society. For every nice, well-meaning street person you may encounter, there will be others that may wish to assault you or steal your belongings. Moreover, police frequently do periodic "roundups" that involve arresting suspected vagrants in large numbers, and these operations usually target areas frequented by transients.

If you hope to avoid encounters with overzealous police, you must strive to keep up your daily appearance. In the larger scheme of things, being cleanly shaved, washed and smelling nice may seem relatively unimportant to someone struggling to eke out an existence without adequate shelter. Yet most people who have been homeless will tell you that maintaining your personal hygiene should be given a high priority. Be sure to wash as often as you can, and take the time to brush your teeth. You don't want to get cavities when you're down on your luck. Along with the salutary health benefits of staying clean, your appearance is of vital importance.

It's a harsh but very real fact that most people rely on stereotypes when interacting with strangers. While we like to think of ourselves as open-minded, most members of the public who encounter someone who is foul-smelling, unkempt and unshaven will immediately place these individuals into unflattering categories like "wino," "mentally ill," "junkie" or "possible criminal." Whether this is right or wrong is beside the point. You must accept that visual discrimination is a fact of life, and people tend to rely on superficial observations when meeting new people. It's depressing, but the human species isn't going to change anytime soon. The fact is that there are a great number of homeless people among us who have jobs, but simply can't afford housing. Yet we are not even aware of their desperate situation because they work tirelessly to maintain a presentable appearance that allows them to move seamlessly through society.

For bathing, if you belong to a gym, don't let your membership lapse, as this may allow you access to a shower facility. In a pinch, you can also go to any gym or YMCA and purchase a day pass if you desperately need to shower. Most camping stores carry solar-heated shower units for under $20. You simply fill the unit with water, leave it in the sun for a while, and when you're ready, open up a small spigot and enjoy a short shower with warm water. Be sure you know an out-of-the-way location where you can take your shower undetected, or you could be arrested for public indecency.

In a worst-case scenario, baby wipes, paper towels and liquid soap can be used in a public bathroom for day-to-day hygiene. Most upscale coffeehouses have bathrooms with locks, so you might try these types of establishments when business is slow if you need to go for a full-scale sponge bath. Large institutions like colleges and libraries will often have bathrooms that are often vacant during off hours. Scout out possible bathing locations carefully, as you don't want to be sponge bathing when there are others who may need to use the restroom. Try not to make a mess. If someone complains about you, you could be banned. Try to keep your clothes clean as well. A few loads at a coin-operated laundromat probably won't cost you more than a few dollars, and will save you a lot of opposition from the general public.

In terms of basic sustenance, you will need to rely on public drinking fountains and restrooms for obtaining water. Food will pose a difficult challenge. If you don't have access to your survival provisions, you can try foraging for edible plants, dumpster diving at restaurants and supermarkets, and obtaining food through soup kitchens or food banks. If you'd like some resources for obtaining food, America's Second Harvest, a non-profit dedicated to feeding the hungry, maintains a listing of food banks across the U.S. on the organization's web page (secondharvest.org). Remember to include a can opener with your possessions—it may come in handy. If you are uncertain about homeless resources in your area and are willing to travel, you may wish to consider a locality such as Seattle, WA or San Francisco, CA, that has well-established programs for assisting the homeless population with clean clothes, soup kitchens and food banks, as well as job and housing referrals.

If you find yourself craving the amenities of civilization, look no further than your local public library for a comfortable chair, endless reading material, free internet, bathroom facilities and, depending on the weather, a warm or cool place to unwind. You can also make the library your base of operations for locating housing and pursuing job leads, maintaining correspondence and keeping in touch with family and friends.

Choosing where to bed down for the night can often be a daunting challenge. Camping is generally forbidden in public parks and many locations, so you will need to think carefully about where you choose to sleep. Let's take a look at a few possible options:

Public Transportation: If you are familiar with public transportation and safety is a primary concern, you can do a lot worse than snoozing on a bus or subway line that runs into the predawn hours (in larger cities there could be safety concerns). As long as you get used to sleeping under the glare of bright lights and not being able to stretch out, you will at least be in a somewhat clean, safe environment. Be sure to use the bathroom before you board. The waiting areas in bus and train stations may also provide temporary shelter, but don't make it a regular habit or you may be asked to leave by security.

Vacant Lots: If you can locate a large vacant lot that isn't directly visible from the street, you might try pitching your tent for a night or two. Keep a low profile. If you plan on returning, try not to make a mess and avoid urinating or defecating, as this will only lead to complaints from neighbors, and police may start monitoring the area.

Outdoor Restrooms: Some businesses and government offices maintain outdoor restrooms that are often kept open during the night. You will need to monitor these locations to find out when the janitors come to clean in the morning, but you can at least enjoy some temporary shelter for a few hours in the evenings so that you can get some rest. The added value of these locations is that you will have immediate access to bathroom facilities. Be warned: You may have to contend with some intolerable smells if the bathrooms get heavy use during the day, and it may not be a good idea during summer.

Natural Cover: Hitchhikers have been known to "stealth camp" in the lush trees and shrubs near freeway on-ramps and roads. A number of shopping malls also have similar vegetation that might provide adequate camouflage, so long as you find an area that receives minimal foot traffic and few people have been known to camp there.

These are just a few suggestions. Keep in mind that as our society becomes more regimented, there will likely be fewer and fewer opportunities for clandestine camping, so you may need to be creative. Try golf courses, college campuses, underneath billboards. Take the time to do a general reconnaissance of your area. You never know what you might find. Wherever you choose to sleep, never make a mess or leave evidence of your presence, and always keep your valuables close by. Violence against the homeless has been rising steadily in recent years, so try to maintain the lowest possible profile. As you will likely be jailed if you carry a handgun, at the very least consider carrying a legal, non-lethal weapon for self-defense, such as a can of mace or pepper spray.

Loneliness is something you must also think about. You may be by yourself for extended periods of time, and there is a good chance your social skills may start to wither. Some people suffering from homelessness start to slowly withdraw from society, and this only makes a bad situation worse. Stay in contact with friends and relatives, and try to find outlets for social interaction. If you're not working, and having trouble finding a new job, consider volunteering. While it may not pay, the experience will add to and sharpen your marketable skills and keep you interacting with the public, and you may make some valuable connections.

Living in Your Car

IF YOU STILL HAVE OWNERSHIP OF YOUR VEHICLE, AND YOU CAN'T find any shelter, living in your car is probably your best option. At the very least, you will have a roof over your head, some storage space, mobility and, depending on the size of your car, a comfortable place to lie down. However, be warned: Most municipalities maintain strictly enforced prohibitions against overnight parking. If you plan on spending the night in your car, you will need to be vigilant about concealing your presence from police and suspicious homeowners.

Perhaps the easiest way to camouflage your roadside slumber from prying eyes is to purchase an inexpensive car cover. When you've found a safe parking spot, and you're ready to bed down for the night, simply place the cover over your car and then slip underneath, lock your door and revel in your anonymity. If it's windy, you may need to use string or bungee cords to secure the cover. If you think the car cover is too cumbersome and you'd like greater visibility, you can also apply tinting to your windows (make sure it's the legal kind) and place a sun guard on the windshield. If you own a van, placing towels or curtains in front of the windows and using a sun guard should also do the trick.

Your anonymity also requires you to keep your car clean. If you plan on parking overnight in a well-to-do neighborhood, pulling up in a dirty, cluttered vehicle will immediately draw suspicion, especially at night. Make sure your important belongings are well-organized and placed in clean bags (which you can get at any supermarket) or sealed plastic containers. If you have access to a hose or there is a coin-operated car wash in your area, clean your car regularly. It will save you a lot of unnecessary problems. If you plan on relying on your food provisions, be sure that these items are packed securely in clean, food-grade containers. If storage is a problem, removing the back seat is an option you should consider. This will extend your storage space and, with some creative arranging, will allow you some added legroom to stretch out.

Evenings are when you will be at your most vulnerable. You will want to avoid both police and thieves. A middle- or lower-middle class residential neighborhood is usually your best option. As long as you have taken adequate measures to conceal your presence inside the vehicle, and your car isn't a complete wreck, you shouldn't encounter too many problems. However, make sure you never park directly in front of someone's home or you will draw immediate attention. Park either midway between two homes or some place that doesn't directly face the front window of a house. Always remember to crack your window, or the condensation will be a dead giveaway. Twenty-four-hour truck stops are another good choice, as the heavy traffic will allow you to blend in without anyone noticing you, and some establishments offer reasonably clean shower facilities that are available for rent by the hour. Wal-Mart locations are generally liberal about overnight parking, so you might want to check and see if any outlets near you will let you park for the night. Campsites and rest stops are also recommended. Some even have public showers.

In terms of what to avoid, steer clear of both seedy urban areas and upscale districts. If you park in a high-crime part of a city or town, you run the risk of your car being broken into or being robbed or carjacked. If you settle in a wealthy section of a town or city, the likelihood of being woken up by either private security guards or police will increase significantly. Never park near schools or any other place where children congregate, or you could find yourself being questioned by police. Stay as far away as you can from police stations, as law enforcement officials tend to closely monitor the surrounding area. You must also make sure you are a good distance from banks and other security-conscious businesses, as these locations are often closely watched by police and your presence will draw immediate attention.

The odds are that at some point you will come into contact with law enforcement. It is important that you never admit to police that you are homeless or living in your vehicle. Doing so will immediately place you at risk of being cited or arrested. Tell them that you are taking a nap after a long drive, en route to a destination, aren't feeling well and decided to rest a bit, etc. Be polite and courteous and promise them that you will be moving along shortly. These responses may not be truthful, but the minute you confess to being homeless, their attitude toward you will change dramatically and you may even be taken into custody for vagrancy, loitering or some other offense. Even if you're a stickler for honesty, don't risk it.

If you'd like a bit of stimulation in the evenings, Coby Electronics offers an affordable, battery-powered black-and-white portable television/radio with a 5" screen for under $20. The small-sized TV also includes a headphone jack if you're worried the noise from your television or radio will alert neighbors to your presence. Check PortableTVs.com for a selection of battery-powered televisions. If you're in a secure location that doesn't require stealth and you'd like some lighting in the evenings, most camping stores carry a wide array of hand-crank and solar-powered lanterns that can easily illuminate your vehicle's interior. A sleeping bag or inexpensive air mattress will also greatly enhance your comfort. Don't become too reliant on microwaveable junk foods. You can obtain an inexpensive Coleman stove at most camping stores that can help with your cooking needs. However, never cook your meals inside your car, and be careful about where you store your fuel, as this poses a very serious fire hazard. Keep in mind that you can also purchase an inverter for your car's DC outlet at Radio Shack that will increase your power and allow you to run a number of smaller appliances.

Most people who have lived in their car for an extended period recommend that you avoid larger cities and stick to small to medium-sized towns. It's usually safer, and you will often find more undeveloped places to park your car overnight that won't draw attention. If you'd like a more comprehensive overview of car-living options, get a copy of *Ten Consecutive Years Living in Cars* by Craig S. Roberts. It's the ultimate bible for the car-living experience.

Squatting

LIVING IN YOUR CAR OR ON THE STREETS AREN'T THE ONLY CHOICES available to those without shelter. In recent years a growing number of homeless Americans have begun engaging in the practice of squatting. In strictly legal terms, squatting is the act of taking up rent-free residence in an abandoned building or unoccupied home without the express permission of the owner. Although the squatter lifestyle is popular in parts of Europe and is viewed as an act of political protest, in the U.S. squatting is considered a form of trespassing or even breaking and entering, and is strongly discouraged by authorities. However, in some locations, like New York, squatters have been known to move in and set up housekeeping in vacant buildings. Indeed, some of the more ingenious squats have running water and electricity, and the residents will carry out extensive renovations to the property.

There are generally two types of squats: "back window" and "front door." The former is generally the most prevalent and involves an individual or group setting up a clandestine housing arrangement in an unoccupied home or building. The de facto residents usually sneak in and out of the property while steering clear of neighbors and staying one step ahead of the owner. Self-styled "gutter punks" and transients tend to favor this method for securing housing.

"Front door" squatters make little effort to hide their presence and will even inform neighbors of their situation in the hopes of building community support. Front door squatting is rooted in the legal doctrine of "adverse possession," which dates back to English common law. According to this centuries-old legal principle, in certain circumstances a squatter can claim ownership of a disputed property without compensating the owner, providing that certain criteria are met—such as maintaining continuous occupancy for a specific number of years, making renovations to the property, an "open and notorious" claim of ownership, and other requirements.

In one of the more successful front door squatting efforts, a group of artists and community activists took over a dilapidated building at 123 Delancey Street on New York's Lowest East Side in 1980 in protest of local land use policies. In response, city officials evicted the squatters but allowed them to occupy another building at 156 Rivington Street, a location that they christened "ABC No Rio." Over the next decade, the squatters resided in a sort of legal gray area, paying a nominal rent to the city but still lacking any sort of legal standing. This situation changed in 1994, when the City of New York revoked ABC No Rio's lease, stopped accepting rent checks and began negotiating a sale of the property to a local non-profit organization. However, in 1997 a compromise was reached allowing the squatters at ABC No Rio to take over ownership of the property for $1 providing the building was brought up to code and extensive renovations were made. City officials later backpedaled and tried to renege on the deal, but in 2006 the agreement was finalized and the artists took over ownership of the property, providing that they complete the requested renovations.

While the ABC No Rio saga will likely serve to inspire other housing activists to set up communitarian front door squats, the majority of American squatters by and large prefer the back window method. Indeed, the foreclosure crisis is offering numerous opportunities for enterprising squatters looking for stealth housing. The combination of a protracted real estate slump and skyrocketing foreclosures has left America dotted with unoccupied homes and buildings.

According to a Reuters article that appeared in May 2008, "squatting is on the rise" throughout the country. In areas blighted by depressed home sales and record foreclosures, squatters are becoming a regular presence. "Foreclosed homes," remarked a real estate broker quoted in the article, "are like a campground with free camping."[2]

While it is difficult to foretell the future, the dismal economic situation could lead to an increase in squatting. A major uptick in fuel prices could also play a role. As suburban homes are abandoned because of lengthy and often expensive commutes, and credit markets tighten, resulting in fewer home sales, the prospect of squatter colonies sprouting in what were once middle-class and upscale communities isn't all that far-fetched. According to a March 2008 article in the *San Francisco Chronicle,* a growing number of urban planners envision the "pristine, newly-built developments of four-bedroom, three-bath dream houses produced in the last housing boom" becoming "ghettos for the poor and disenfranchised."[3]

If you should face a desperate situation where squatting may provide your only viable means of shelter, you must keep in mind that you will be breaking the law, and if you are apprehended by police you could be prosecuted for trespassing and possibly other crimes, such as vandalism and breaking and entering. If you plan on setting up a squat, take the time to research how your locality deals with people occupying abandoned homes or buildings. In some cities, squatters are simply evicted, while in others the full force of the law is brought to bear and you could be looking at jail time. Unless you intimately know everyone involved, avoid group squats if you can. Some urban squats can become particularly violent, and if there is heavy drug use going on, the police will intervene at some point and you won't just be evicted, you may be arrested on drug charges.

Most squatters advise that you maintain the property as if you owned it. Authorities will be less likely to charge you with trespassing if you haven't damaged or vandalized the home or building. It's also important that you keep a low profile and avoid conflict with neighbors. If you run across someone, be courteous and polite, and you may be viewed as just another resident. Many squatters believe that city-owned properties make better squats, as it is far more difficult for the city to evict you than would a private owner.

If you'd like more information about squatting, Freegan.info, a web page for sustainable living tips, offers an informative online guide for would-be American squatters. Squatter City is also an excellent blog that covers squatting activities through the world (squattercity.blogspot.com). Although it is a UK-based site, Squat.net has some valuable information about squatting practices and the surrounding legal issues.

Homeless, but on the Move

IF YOU'RE THE ADVENTUROUS TYPE, THERE ARE ADDITIONAL ROADS you can take if you should find yourself without shelter. If you have a little money and would like to put your financial life on hold for a short while, there are a few interesting avenues you can explore that might be well worth your time. Let's take a look at a few:

The Couch Surfing Project: CSP is a free, international online service that allows members to register and request room and board from members across the world. Hundreds of thousands of members in dozens of countries are offering hospitality and accommodations to registered couch surfers. Sometimes it's entirely free of charge; sometimes you may have to reimburse your host for minor expenses. You co-ordinate your stay with a registered CSP member, and then you can travel to your destination without worrying about finding a place to stay or dining in expensive restaurants. If you like to travel, this is an amazing way to visit other cities or countries at a reduced cost. Check out CouchSurfing.com for more information.

House Sitting: If you're responsible and well-organized, and enjoy housekeeping, there are homeowners throughout the world who will let you stay in their homes rent-free while they are away in exchange for upkeep, lawn and garden care, feeding and caring for pets, etc. Some owners may require a security deposit, and some may pay a weekly salary or for certain specialized services like bill-paying and repairs. The practice is becoming increasingly common due to the advent of the internet. Web pages like HouseCarers.com charge a fee, but allow you to advertise your services to homeowners across the globe. You can also find job leads by subscribing to the Caretaker Gazette (Caretaker.org). Experience and excellent references are a major plus in the house sitting trade, so you may want to stick to simple, rent-free arrangements for your first few house-sitting jobs while you build up your résumé.

Intentional Communities: Intentional Community is a new buzzword describing a growing number of alternative living arrangements that include self-sustaining ecovillages, group and student housing collectives, communes and urban group living projects, residential land trusts and cohabiting spiritual fellowships. Most are very open to visitors, and there are ICs sprinkled across the United States. Spending time traveling across the country and visiting IC communities might make for an interesting low rent road trip if you'd like to experience alternative community living. The Federation for Intentional Community (FIC) has information about the nation's IC communities on the organization's web page (IC.org). Be sure to contact each community and let them know when you plan on visiting so that they can make arrangements. If you're a friendly type with a sociologically curious bent, this might make for a fascinating experience. Who knows? You may find that alternative community living might be a good short- or long-term living option during economic hard times.

National Parks: Retirees have been making this trek for decades: a tour of the nation's National Parks. Obviously this strategy will be highly dependent on gasoline prices, but if you can talk a few friends or family members into coming along and helping with expenses, this should significantly reduce the cost. Most park facilities have showers and restrooms, camping areas, places to buy food and a host of other conveniences. If you're going to be homeless, why not travel the country and enjoy some picturesque scenery? Consult the web page for the National Park Service for more information (NPS.gov).

However you choose to live, always keep in mind that homelessness does not preclude happiness. Perhaps the road-hardened tramp of the industrial age was on to something. He may have been penniless and spent his nights sleeping in hobo jungles and freight cars, but he tried to make the best of his situation and live life to the fullest. Why not ride out the economic storm taking a self-guided tour of the country or trying out an alternative living arrangement? You certainly won't be alone. Thousands of Americans throughout the country live a peripatetic existence on the fringes of society, eking out a basic living but storing invaluable memories of sublime places and fascinating people. You might not earn a lot of money, but as the Park Rangers like to say, you'll get paid in sunsets.

The suggestions listed above are just the tip of the iceberg. •

Notes

1   Armour, Stephanie. "Hitting Home: New Face of Homelessness," *USA Today*, June 26, 2008.

2   Szep, Jason. "As Homes Foreclose in U.S., Squatters Move In," Reuters, May 19, 2008.

3   Lloyd, Carol. "Mortgage Crisis is Creating New 'Slumburbs,'" *San Francisco Chronicle*, March 16, 2008.

CHAPTER 9

WHEN GREENBACKS GO BAD

SURVIVING A CURRENCY CRISIS

When Greenbacks Go Bad:
Surviving a Currency Crisis

WHILE THE DOLLAR ENJOYS AN ALMOST ICONIC STATUS IN THE world's financial markets, we often forget that, like all fiat currencies, it lacks any sort of intrinsic value. In other words, the underlying worth of the money in our bank accounts and wallets rests upon little more than investor confidence in our nation's long-term health. Should this confidence ever be severely tested, the dollar's value could rapidly diminish. Indeed, when suspicions begin to mount that a nation's economy is unsound or its government is incapable of paying its debts, a panicked sell-off can occur. As investors rush toward the exits, the currency loses significant value, and the initial fears that started the panic become a dangerous self-fulfilling prophecy.

Mexico's 1994 peso crisis, triggered by investor concerns over an uprising in the southern state of Chiapas and then-President Ernesto Zedillo's decision to devalue the nation's currency, offers a good example of how a stable fiat currency can run dangerously aground in a very short time. There are already ominous signs the dollar has lost much of its luster. Since 2002, when one dollar was equal to one Euro, the dollar has lost over 20% of its value when compared to other foreign currencies. As of January 2009, one Euro was equal to $1.29. However, during the protracted dollar slump that occurred throughout much of 2008, one Euro could fetch as much as $1.47. When a currency loses value that quickly, it is often symptomatic of a growing unease by foreign investors.

While the recent financial crisis has allowed the dollar to make something of a comeback as foreign central banks and wary investors have gravitated toward U.S. Treasury bonds to ride out the economic storm, we simply cannot be certain that this trend will continue indefinitely. International concerns over America's gargantuan debt load, reckless borrowing, skyrocketing current account deficit and sluggish economic growth have become a regular topic of discussion in the foreign financial press. For the first time since the Second World War, the dollar's status as the world's reserve currency is being openly questioned.

On January 23, 2009, Japanese financial analyst Kosuke Takahashi warned that the U.S. may "give in to the temptation" of "loosening money to feed debt bubbles," and writes that "investors are well advised to diversify their currency positions to hedge against dollar risk."[1] This sentiment is echoed by William Buiter, a professor at the London School of Economics. The economic policy-maker minced no words in a lengthy January 5, 2009 posting on the influential *Financial Times* blog. "There will, before long (my best guess between two and five years from now) be a global dumping of U.S. dollar assets, including U.S. government assets," he predicted. "The U.S. dollar and U.S. Treasury bonds are still viewed as a safe haven by many. But learning takes place."[2]

While we can certainly hope that the dollar will regain its former strength, and effective policies will check its recent downward slide, any undue optimism should be balanced with a certain amount of pragmatism. We simply can't be certain the federal government won't seek to drastically inflate the currency to offset its excessive debts. There is also the possibility that a series of unforeseen events could cause a major sell-off of dollar-denominated securities. Day-to-day life when a currency is in decline can be increasingly hard for consumers. It might be worthwhile to look into how you might cope with a depreciated currency.

Currency in Crisis

UNLESS YOU HAVE THE FUNDS TO PAY $30 OR MORE FOR A CUP OF coffee and drop a month's pay on a trip to the grocery store, your options will be severely limited in terms of purchasing power if a currency crisis should materialize. This is why stocking up on emergency food provisions and other valuable supplies, as we've recommended in previous chapters, is a worthwhile strategy during periods of economic instability.

Individuals who have suffered through a monetary crisis frequently cite the inability to make any sort of financial plans when everything is in constant flux. Each morning, every headline in the financial press is closely scrutinized for how each day's events will affect the falling currency. In his insightful study of money, historian Jack Weatherford describes what he calls a "peculiar inflation culture" that developed during Bolivia's economic crisis of the 1980s. "Every business, from the large national airline to the woman selling shelled nuts on the street corner," he explains, "must know the value of the peso relative to that of the dollar at all times of the day and must play a constant game of shuffling pesos, dollars and goods."[3]

Fortunately, with some initiative and ingenuity, people can learn to adapt to living in a society without a viable form of money. When Argentina's peso collapsed, citizens relied on what the locals call *trueque,* a Spanish word for barter or exchange. In 2001, the currency was devalued by an estimated 70% and the Argentine government converted bank accounts denominated in dollars to next-to-worthless pesos. Savings were wiped out and withdrawals were limited to pension payments and government salaries. Fortunately, barter provided a much-needed alternative to a desperate public. "If you don't have any money, this is the only way to survive," Irma Gonzales, an unemployed secretary informed *Time* magazine in May 2002.[4]

As the Argentine economy went into deep recession, public bartering became a regular occurrence in twenty of Argentina's 24 provinces, with 450 different barter clubs in active operation. Through these community swap networks, consumers could trade for a wide array of goods ranging from farm produce to skincare products to hand-sewn clothing. Soon, unemployed professionals from the nation's newly impoverished middle classes began plying their respective trades in exchange for food and other badly needed household goods.

"This is not a living, but it keeps me and my family above water," Pedro Perez, a semi-employed manager of a shoe factory told a *New York Times* reporter in 2001.[5] While his employers could no longer afford to pay his entire salary, the shoes and other items he received in lieu of money allowed the 43-year-old to trade his meager wares for "fruits, vegetables and hand-made clothes."

What began as a social experiment quickly evolved into a valuable community-based economy. Relying on word of mouth, the internet and public advertisements, at the height of the crisis an estimated six million active traders took part in some form of barter.[6] Some of the clubs even began exchanging a form of scrip known as *creditos* that could be freely exchanged for goods and services. To protect the fledgling currency against counterfeiters, the barter notes were designed with watermarks capable of being digitally verified as valid community scrip.

Although bartering has fallen off now that Argentina's economy is recovering, the sheer sophistication of the nation's successful *trueque* system offers a possible preview of what life in America might be like should we experience a pronounced dollar crisis and consumer purchasing power is severely depleted. While few people got rich, Argentina's amazingly resilient consumers were provided a much-needed economic outlet that kept many families from falling into desperate poverty. At its peak, barter become so prevalent that *creditos* even began to seep into the nation's mainstream economy, with local suppliers accepting the community cash in lieu of pesos.

An American Tradition

SOME OBSERVERS DESCRIBED ARGENTINA'S EXPERIMENTAL POST-cash economy as a historic return to the bartering practices that prevailed among pre-Columbian civilizations. Although it doesn't stretch back as far, America also has a long and venerable history of barter. While we like to romanticize our frontier antecedents as stubborn individualists who were self-reliant in every facet of life, the reality was that swapping produce, tools and consumer goods was vital to early American economic life. As barter historian Annie Proulx writes, "Only through communal efforts, exchanging work and swapping and trading surplus goods and skills, were the colonists able to provide for themselves, and eventually, over several generations, to build up thriving homesteads."[7]

Many colonial-era crops, like hemp, timber and tobacco, were specifically cultivated for barter. Community swaps became even more prevalent when the vast agricultural holdings of the 17th and 18th centuries were subsequently sold off and divided into smaller farms. The separation of pastureland, woodlots and hayfields made bartering available resources a precondition to operating a successful farm. Proulx contends that these cashless transactions provided the means to maintain "the efficiency and self-containment of the large old farm."[8]

This enduring tradition of barter would undergo a major resurgence in the early 20th century, when the Great Depression-era cash crunch swept through rural America. By offering produce in lieu of money, moneyless farmers were able to hire field hands to help harvest crops. Thousands of farmers, workers and tradesmen subsequently formed barter leagues in a half dozen agricultural states that were instrumental in easing the privations of the Great Depression.

Unfortunately, barter never quite caught on in America's cities. In the 1930s, most urban residents were employed in specialized occupations that weren't easily transferable to a barter economy. For example, an unemployed clerical worker, machinist or train engineer would have difficulty bartering his skills at a time when people's greatest needs tended to revolve around the essentials—food, shelter, clothing, etc. Moreover, sprawling urban locales often lacked the level of co-operation and pervasive bartering culture found in tight-knit rural communities. However, much has changed in the intervening years. As evidenced by the role that Argentina's cities played in the nation's cash-free economy, advancements in communications and network technology have eliminated many of these barriers.

The Digital Marketplace

PERHAPS WE CAN CONSIDER OURSELVES FORTUNATE THAT A RUDI-mentary bartering marketplace is already in existence. Web pages like Craigslist.com, SwapTree.com, WebSwap.com and SwapThing.com allow traders to connect online and carry out barter exchanges to obtain a diverse variety of products and services. As the nation's economic troubles mounted in the latter part of 2008, there were already signs that barter was becoming a viable option for cost-conscious American consumers. As of July 2008, there were an estimated 142,000 items listed in the barter section on Craigslist. Susan MacTavish Best, a spokesperson for Craigslist, informed CNN that the number of barter postings had doubled compared to last year's figures.[9] "When the economy turns unfriendly, Craigslist users become far more creative to get their everyday tasks done," she observed.

The internet seems destined to play a key role in shaping and advancing America's barter economy. Hundreds of organizations and companies now provide online applications to facilitate greater trading among businesses and consumers. The Northern California-based SwapThing.com, for example, offers free registration and listings for traders. The site provides a helpful search engine for traders looking to obtain a specific product or service, and the company behind Swap Thing has even started a Swap Affiliate program that allows community and social networking sites to host small-scale barter exchanges in neighborhoods throughout the U.S. This decentralized approach, which relies on existing social networks, could prove vital in the event of a serious currency collapse. Again, your ability to cultivate a rich and diverse social network should play an important role in your economic survival strategy. The more people know about your bartering efforts, the more likely you will attract a marketplace for your goods.

If you'd prefer something a bit more sophisticated, sites like BarterBucks. us offer an estimated fifty million products available for trade, and allow users to purchase items by using the credits received from traded goods. Although many sites like these charge a nominal fee for each transaction, and some charge a membership fee, the benefits of using a barter-based currency may outweigh these costs.

While the proliferation of online swap sites has produced a unique long-tailed market for everything from appliances to vacations, in September 2008 *Trend Central*, an online publication that monitors evolving changes in consumer behavior, reported a growth in food-related swaps on the internet. Whether motivated by a need to scale back waste or to avoid the high cost of groceries, *Trend Central* researchers detected a spike in "message board postings with offers of food giveaways, shares and swaps."[10] The article predicts the growth of "Craigslist-style" web pages that "connect consumers who want to swap and barter using cuisine as currency."

Another innovative concept that's gaining traction is "time banking." Members of a community will launch a time bank web page where members create profiles and a list of services they would be willing to do for free—like walking dogs, cutting hair, watering plants or changing someone's oil. Every hour you volunteer is the equivalent of a "time dollar" that is credited to your account. These can be cashed in whenever you need someone to help you out. All you need to do is search through the individual profiles until you find someone offering a service you might need. The more people who volunteer, the more services are available to the community. It's also a great way to connect and build ties with your neighbors. If you're interested in starting a time bank in your area, take a look at the Time Banks web page for more information (timebanks.org).

The internet isn't the only game in town. If you'd prefer to do your trading face-to-face, there are barter sections in many newspapers and local publications. If your area doesn't have any barter opportunities, it will be up to you to take the initiative. Posting flyers and notices on community bulletin boards might be a good way to advertise. You might also consider attending any swap meets that congregate in your area. These are the kind of gatherings that will form the nucleus of a barter-based economy, and person-to-person bartering might be more interesting than making your trades online.

Marketing

IF YOU WERE FORCED TO RELY ON COMMUNITY BARTER TO SUPPLE-ment your income, what kinds of products or services would you offer? Keep in mind that consumer demands will be radically altered should the U.S. suffer the convulsions of a protracted currency crisis. Foods and household goods we take for granted may be scarce and much in demand. Luxury items and modern conveniences could become increasingly difficult to obtain. Fuel shortages (which tend to accompany currency crises) could limit your mobility, and the casual trip to the mall may be out of the question. If you're unsure of where to begin, we've included a few general recommendations below:

Boarding: Record foreclosures and a shortage of available housing could place a premium on living situations. Scaling back your lifestyle and taking in a boarder in exchange for food, renovations or assistance with a home-based business or bartering project might be a good idea during difficult times. Likewise, bartering with your landlord to provide renovations, upkeep or maintenance to the building in exchange for living rent-free might be an opportunity worth pursuing.

Caretaking/Security: Economic hard times will cause a spike in property crimes. If you have a background in house sitting, security or law enforcement, you may be able to set up a barter situation for room and board in exchange for acting as a caretaker or security guard at someone's home or apartment. You might also be able to work out a similar arrangement with local businesses in exchange for trade goods you can barter.

Gardening: Food shortages and exorbitant grocery costs will give a decisive trading advantage to those who have access to fresh produce. Consider setting up an extensive backyard or urban garden, renting space at a community garden, or working out an arrangement with a local farm. Local Harvest is a great resource for information about small-scale farming in your area (localharvest.org/csa). Raising rabbits, chickens or pigeons for meat is another option. You can barter with other home cultivators or swap your surplus food with another trader. If you have extensive experience, teaching people how to grow their own fruits and vegetables is another possible trading option.

Home Production: When high consumer prices and limited imports keep people from going to the malls, skilled artisans who can make durable, handmade clothing, pottery, furniture and other goods will become an important community resource. If you're good at arts and crafts, sewing or woodwork, this might be a viable trading enterprise. Stocking up on inexpensive but durable thrift-store clothing, learning to mend old clothes, or knitting or crocheting blankets and scarves are other options.

Liquor: When the economy goes into the tank, disconnecting from reality or at least enjoying a temporary respite from the world's financial troubles will be a serious temptation for many people. In other words, there might be a serious demand for booze. If you've dabbled with microbrews, selling homemade beer or wine could be a profitable endeavor. When the Russian ruble collapsed, homebrewed liquor became a thriving concern, and there's little reason to believe America will be any different.

Sundries: If the currency goes into the tank, high prices will likely make some of the items we rely upon for our daily needs unaffordable. Amassing a stockpile of things like soap and shampoo, medicines, toilet paper, toothpaste, Band-Aids, Q-Tips, diapers, batteries and other products might make for a good bartering strategy.

These are just a few basic suggestions. Your trading efforts will be dependent on several factors, such as the extent of the currency crisis, availability of fuel and imported products, and the consumer culture within your community. Obviously, selling booze in the Bible Belt will go over about as well as offering freshly slaughtered meat in a vegetarian enclave of San Francisco. Keep in mind that barter is more an art than a science, and each trade has its own unique characteristics. However, there are a few guidelines you might want to keep in mind.

For one thing, never be afraid to make an offer. Even if your swap proposal is turned down, you might learn that your fellow trader is specifically looking for something you have access to, and a revised swap might work. If you plan on advertising on a barter site or community bulletin board, you should also remember to be as detailed as possible in describing what you are offering for trade. Posting a photo of your product is usually a good idea. The less information you provide, the more likely you will end up answering innumerable questions from curious browsers.

You should also consider estimating the value (either in dollars or swap credits) of what you plan on bartering. Even if economic circumstances force people to engage in cash-free transactions, people want to have a basic understanding of what something is worth. You must also keep in mind that the Internal Revenue Service considers any barter transaction that involves a profit to be a form of taxable income, so you might want to focus on equitable trades to avoid any unnecessary hassle from the government. You should also try to think of ways you can barter existing resources. Trade futures on your backyard lemon tree. If you have an extensive book or CD collection, create a barter-based lending library. Barter your spare bedroom to visiting tourists. Whatever assets or abilities you have can be bartered.

Opting Out

AS IT WAS INSTITUTED IN 1913, ONE OF THE PRIMARY DUTIES OF THE Federal Reserve was to ensure price stability. Unfortunately, the Fed seems to have lost sight of this primary mission. Indeed, most of us have spent our entire adult lives chasing after a forever-rising cost of living. To a deficit-be-damned politician, near-constant inflation is a fine thing. It cheapens government debt and increases tax revenue by pushing people into higher tax brackets. Wall Street has also reaped huge benefits from inflation, as the easy flow of money and credit provides the necessary capital for increased financial speculation. However, these inflated dollars caused by the Fed's loose currency policies do little for the average consumer. If anything, the flow of cheap dollars makes our lives harder as we are forced to contend with diminished buying power and constantly rising prices. For this reason, many liken inflation to a "stealth tax," as a debased currency extracts wealth from us by depleting the value of our savings and forcing us to pay more for goods and services.

Alternative currencies are a possible way for consumers to opt out of our nation's mismanaged currency system and get more value for their money. Moreover, these innovative units of exchange are particularly useful during economic hard times—whether caused by a deflationary cash crunch or a period of sustained inflation. "When money gets dried up and there are still needs to be met in society, people come up with creative ways to meet those needs." explains Peter North, a currency historian at the University of Liverpool, in a December 14, 2008 interview with *Time* magazine.[11] Indeed, during the Great Depression there were literally thousands of alternative currencies in circulation as the nation struggled with a protracted deflation.

Micro-currency advocates believe that by unplugging from the often-volatile global currency system, communities become more economically resilient while ensuring that existing capital goes toward supporting local businesses. Perhaps most importantly, many of these small-scale initiatives help foster a greater sense of community. However, this is not to say that there is any single model for community currencies; there are dozens of existing models. While some rely on sophisticated software and conduct transactions over the internet, others are limited to a small city or district and involve a limited number of participants.

The latter model was adopted by a group of residents in Ithaca, NY when the community was impacted by the 1991 recession. The local currency is called Ithaca Hours (ithacahours.org). The non-profit initiative currently has over 900 participants, who use the script valued at $10 for each Ithaca Hour. Participants who are business owners agree to allow a certain percentage of their revenues to be paid with Ithaca Hours. Likewise, employee participants receive a portion of their wages in the community currency, which keeps their earnings circulating in the local economy. The Ithaca Hours community board also extends loans to small businesses. While both employees and business owners must still rely on cash transactions for certain expenses, this innovative medium of exchange has gained a permanent economic foothold, and may become an important community asset during Depression 2.0.

Berkshares (berkshares.org) is another type of alternative currency that has experienced significant growth since the E.F. Schumacher Society introduced it in 2006. The organization, which is based in western Massachusetts, has partnered with over 350 businesses that now accept the community scrip in lieu of dollars. Berkshare activists have also formed partnerships with local banks. There are now twelve separate banking locations where consumers can exchange their cash for Berkshares. To provide incentive, all participating businesses offer a ten percent discount to any consumer who pays in community currency. For example, if you were to purchase a $100 pair of high-tops at an affiliated sporting goods store, you would only be paying $90 if you paid with Berkshares. After just two years, an estimated two million Berkshares are now in circulation.

The Community Exchange System or CES (www.ces.org.za) is perhaps the most ambitious attempt to move away from what its advocates call the "usury-based global money system." This internet-based effort seeks to harness technology to create a means of exchanging goods and services "without using conventional currencies" and "build a sense of community at the same time." Consumers register with the program online and are given an account number and a password. However, there are also CES branches for consumers who may lack internet access. No money is needed to start an account. The way it works, by buying or providing services or goods to fellow participants through the site's "offerings list," you generate either debits or credits that are entered in your account. To avoid abuses of the system, everyone's trading information is made public.

To give an example of how CES works, let's suppose you agreed to repair someone's computer for an agreed upon number of credits. Once you've performed the service to the satisfaction of your customer, you log the transaction into your account as a credit. Conversely, your customer logs the transaction in his account as a debit. While you can use your credits to purchase a good or service, your client must provide a similar community service or sell something of similar value to clear the debit from his or her account. As the system is global, you can spend your credits virtually anywhere in the world. There are already an estimated 119 community exchange networks operating in nineteen countries.

These are just a few examples of how community currencies can provide an alternative to Federal Reserve notes. While these efforts have yet to completely capture the public imagination, who knows what the future holds? The first initial efforts to create a barter economy in Argentina in the mid-1990s received a lukewarm reception, but economic hard times transformed a small, grassroots initiative into a cultural phenomenon.

At least for now, the dollar remains the primary medium of exchange. However, a serious dollar crisis may cause radical changes in how we transact business with barter, community currencies and other alternatives entering the mainstream. It might be a good idea to familiarize yourself with whatever alternatives are available in your community or, better yet, start your own. If you'd like more information about community currencies, the Complimentary Currency Resource Center is an excellent starting point (complementarycurrency.org). •

Notes

1   Takahashi, Kosuke. "The Temptation of Dollar Seigniorage," *Asia Times*, January 23, 2009.

2   Buiter, William. "Can the U.S. Economy Afford a Keynesian Stimulus?," *Financial Times* blog, January 5, 2009.

3   Weatherford, Jack. *The History of Money,* (New York: Three Rivers Press, 1997). p. 198.

4   Katel, Peter. "Argentina: The Post-Money Economy," *Time*, February 5, 2002.

5   Krauss, Clifford. "To Weather Recession, Argentines Revert to Barter," *New York Times*, May 5, 2001.

6   Sad, Elizabeth L. "Argentina: Barter Clubs," *Toward Freedom*, March 2004.

7   Proulx, Annie. *What'll You Take For It?: Back to Barter,* (Garden Way: Vermont, 1981). p. 13.

8   Ibid., p. 3.

9   Pawlowski, A. "No Cash? No Problem, If You Barter," CNN.com, September 2, 2008.

10 "The Latest Trend in Food: Food Swapping," *Trend Central*, September 22, 2008.

11 Schwartz, Judith D. "Alternative Currencies Grow in Popularity," *Time*, December 14, 2008.

CHAPTER 10

SURVIVAL FINANCES
INVESTMENTS FOR AN
UNCERTAIN FUTURE

Survival Finances: Investments for an Uncertain Future

IN THE TENSION-FILLED MONTHS AHEAD, DON'T BE SURPRISED IF YOU run across dozens of book titles, videos and high-priced investment seminars promising various "sure-fire" strategies to "cash in" on the current crisis. Be sure to keep in mind that these kinds of aggressively-promoted investment tips played no small role in our current economic predicament. Some of the same familiar faces who urged us "go long on tech stocks" in the 1990s, or who spent the last few years touting the "red-hot" real estate market will be resurfacing to peddle some newfangled "depression-proof" investment trend—with the same results.

The wholesale destruction of personal assets is one of the most traumatic consequences of a severe economic crisis. If you can emerge from the wreckage with your balance sheet relatively intact, then you've come out ahead. The primary focus of this book is economic survival, and this chapter will be limited to outlining a few general investment options and possible strategies to safeguard your wealth at a time of pronounced uncertainty.

The month-to-month trajectory of Depression 2.0 will be subject to a great deal of speculation. Like medieval theologians debating a disputed scriptural passage, government economists, financial commentators and other market experts will be arguing endlessly over the exact status of the economy. Are we experiencing inflation, deflation or possibly stagflation? These are important concepts to know, as they will greatly impact how you choose to protect your assets. Before we discuss investment options, let's take a moment and briefly examine each of these terms.

Deflation

The massive deleveraging and worldwide credit crunch that signaled the onset of Depression 2.0 has been characterized by a protracted deflation, which is traditionally defined as a reduction in the amount of available cash or credit relative to the total number of available goods and services. When money is scarce, we can expect an overall decline in prices, spending, production and investment. As companies cut jobs to reduce overhead and shore up flagging balance sheets, unemployment and layoffs increase. This creates what 20th-century British economist John Maynard Keynes called a "liquidity trap"—worried consumers reduce spending and, in response, businesses cut jobs and investments. This dangerous negative feedback loop can often prove difficult to break.

To counter deflation, central banks will usually increase the amount of money in circulation by extending loans at below-market rates to banks, providing emergency funding to troubled companies and financial firms, and lowering interest rates to encourage borrowing and investment. Governments will also intervene by providing tax cuts and start-up funds to businesses and creating jobs through initiatives akin to President Roosevelt's public works projects during the Great Depression. These kinds of measures are currently being contemplated as a possible solution to Depression 2.0.

A deflation is generally considered the worst possible atmosphere for investing. Because prices are low and consumer spending drops, corporate dividends are slashed and stock prices lose significant value. Commodities like oil and precious metals are also impacted as industrial and consumer demand generally fall off when money is tight and the outlook looks bleak. Your investing options will be limited as long as a deflationary environment prevails.

Inflation

INFLATION IS THE COUNTERPART TO DEFLATION, AND CAN OFTEN prove just as difficult to manage. The onset of inflation is generally characterized by an upward trend in prices over a sustained period of time. The textbook definition of inflation is an increase in the amount of available cash or credit relative to the total number of available goods and services. During an inflationary period, the purchasing power of a nation's currency will generally erode and is usually reflected in a rising cost of living. Because petroleum is denominated in dollars, an inflated currency can be particularly hard on

American consumers as oil-producing nations will often increase prices to offset the dollar's declining value. This is what Americans experienced during the first part of 2008, when prices spiked for everything from groceries to the cost of commuting to work.

Sometimes an economic boom can lead to inflation as a major increase in employment, wages and salaries will create a greater demand for consumer goods that drives up prices. However, in most instances an inflated currency can be attributed to a poorly-conceived economic policy that favors short-term economic growth over long-term stability. As we've mentioned, politicians also have an incentive to inflate the currency, as a loose monetary policy lowers government operating costs and cheapens outstanding debts. As Ernest Hemingway once wrote, "The first panacea for a mismanaged nation is inflation of the currency."

When governments are unable to service existing loans and run the risk of going into default, the temptation to "monetize" outstanding debts by merely printing the money owed to bondholders or lenders can trigger an uncontrolled inflationary period that is known as "hyperinflation." As the runaway inflation climbs into double and triple digits, consumer savings are often wiped out and businesses go under, because it becomes impossible to borrow money or make a profit with a rapidly fluctuating currency.

Whether the current crisis will enter a period of inflation remains to be seen, but as we've experienced in the past, the federal government has every incentive to drive up inflation. Moreover, because of the exigencies of the financial crisis, the Federal Reserve has overseen an unprecedented expansion in the nation's money supply that could set the stage for a whiplash-like wave of inflation.

While many believe the government will be able to spend our way out of the current crisis through various stimulus packages and job-creation initiatives, this kind of deficit spending can have a serious impact. Some of the worst inflationary periods in U.S. history occurred in the wake of increased government spending. In the period prior to and following the First World War, the wartime 1940s and the 1970s, excessive government outlays drove inflation to record heights.

Investing when inflation is running high is yet another difficult proposition. As businesses contend with higher operating costs, profits drop and investor enthusiasm wanes when stocks are perceived as overpriced. During the 1970s, when inflation ran into double digits, the stock market fared poorly. When the currency is unstable or inflated, investors generally gravitate toward investments like precious metals and commodities, and some even move their assets into foreign currencies that possess more long-term stability. Bonds are also avoided, as they rarely perform well enough to compete with the rate of inflation. Even keeping your money in the bank can prove hazardous to your assets when the currency is in decline, as the value of your money will erode and interest rates rarely keep up with the rate of inflation.

Stagflation

STAGFLATION IS NOT AN ENVIABLE SCENARIO, AND IS CHARACTERIZED by slow (or non-existent) economic growth, rising unemployment and high levels of inflation. At least in a deflationary environment consumers can look forward to lower prices and increased savings. However, when stagflation prevails, money and credit will be scarce, but overall costs will continue to rise.

When we look back on the history of the 1970s, we often think of Watergate, the Vietnam War and the energy crisis. Yet we often forget that inflation and the rising cost of living were the most pressing concerns for the majority of Americans. Indeed, these issues were paramount during the 1980 presidential elections. Consumers at that time were fearful that inflation would continue to eat away at disposable income and lead to increased poverty. We got a brief taste of stagflation in the first half of 2008 when the economy started to stall but prices continued to climb. Investing when the economy is crippled by stagflation is not unlike the inflationary situation we discussed. Generally, people will move toward precious metals and will studiously avoid stocks and bonds which rarely produce earnings that outpace the rate of inflation.

Cash

LET'S BEGIN OUR SURVEY OF INVESTMENT POSSIBILITIES WITH THE simplest of options: keeping your money in the bank. When the stock market is volatile, companies are going bankrupt, and cases of investor fraud are rising, it might be a good idea to simply park your money in an account, allow your savings to accrue and wait for better times to invest your money. So long as the current crisis is characterized by deflation, you needn't worry about your assets losing value. Moreover, if your money is deposited in an institution insured by the Federal Deposit Insurance Corporation (FDIC), your assets are covered. The FDIC currently insures checking, savings and even CD accounts for up to $250,000 per depositor. If you check the FDIC web page (fdic.gov), you will also find that there are even Individual Retirement Accounts (IRAs) that are insured for up to $250,000. If your deposits aren't above the insured limit and your accounts are under the umbrella of the FDIC, you should be covered if your bank goes under.

While we can certainly take comfort in the knowledge that no one has ever lost a penny depositing money in an FDIC-insured account, we shouldn't ignore the sorry state of America's banking institutions. A 2009 analysis by Goldman Sachs estimates that the banking sector currently holds an estimated $4 trillion in toxic mortgage and consumer debts.[1] The FDIC could be dangerously undercapitalized should the nation's banks be plunged into insolvency. While the federal government has repeatedly reassured the public that our money is safe, and will likely spare no expense to ensure that banks remain solvent, it might be a good idea to pay close attention to the financial status of your bank. Weiss Ratings maintains a listing of the strongest and weakest banking systems online at weissratings.com, and you may want to use this as a guide to choosing a safe place to deposit your money.

If you have significant savings deposits and are worried about the vulnerability of your assets, you might also consider using the Certificate of Deposit Account Registry Service (CDARS), which allows consumers to make sizeable deposits and still enjoy FDIC protection. You sign a Deposit Placement Agreement at an agreed-upon interest rate with a CDARS-affiliated institution nearest you. Your money is then split into several CD accounts and transferred to a number of different CDARS member banks in amounts below FDIC limits, giving your assets complete protection. All of your transactions and statements will be conducted at one CDARS location so you won't have the inconvenience of monitoring several accounts simultaneously. The CDARS web page can be found online at cdars.com.

Dollars in Decline

WHILE KEEPING YOUR MONEY IN THE BANK MIGHT BE A GOOD IDEA in a deflationary environment, should inflation become prevalent, your hard-earned savings could significantly erode in value. For example, if you put your money in a savings or CD account that pays you one or two percent interest, and the rate of inflation is running into double digits, the real-world worth of your savings will be significantly diminished.

Pay close attention to the dollar index, which can be found in the financial section of most newspapers, or online at futures.tradingcharts.com/chart/US/M. The index measures the dollar's relative worth against a basket of foreign currencies. When the index was first instituted in 1973, the value of the dollar was set at 100.0. In the intervening years, the dollar has surged as high as 160.0, but in March 2008 the greenback hit a low point of just over 70. While the dollar has subsequently rebounded, if it starts dipping back into the 70s it's a good sign that investor confidence is weakening. You should also keep a close eye on the Consumer Price Index (CPI), which measures the average cost of a basket of consumer goods. When prices are trending upwards, it's usually a pretty good indication that the dollar is losing purchasing power. The Bureau of Labor Statistics (BLS), a department of the Bureau of Labor, maintains the CPI; current figures can be found online at www.bls.gov/CPI.

If the dollar starts sliding, consider taking precautions. If you have access to a community currency, consider allocating some of your savings to a local money source or possibly diversifying your holdings with a stronger foreign currency that will retain value over time. Take the time to familiarize yourself with which currencies are the most resistant to market fluctuations. Focus on nations that have high rates of consumer savings and fiscally conservative governments. For example, some experts believe the Swiss Franc (CHF) and Singapore Dollar (SGD) will tend to enjoy long-term stability. Most major foreign currencies can easily be purchased at the money conversion counters found in most large airports. However you may want to investigate privacy currency exchanges in your area as the rates at most airports may not be as competitive.

Everbank (everbank.com) is one of the few North American banks that offers FDIC-insured CD and Money Market accounts denominated in major international currencies if you'd like to ensure the safety of your foreign currency holdings. iIf a chosen currency appreciates against the dollar, you stand to earn a small profit. However, if the currency you choose should tank or the dollar rallies, it may cost you a bit of money. Investigate your options carefully—and it might be a good idea to diversify your overseas currency holdings.

Gold

FOR DECADES, GOLD HAS BEEN THE FAVORED ACE IN THE HOLE FOR many conservatively-minded investors—and it's easy to see why. While fiat currencies may come and go, gold will never lose its status as a universally recognized store of value. For the better part of the mid-20th century, the average price of gold rarely exceeded $35 an ounce. Year in and year out, the legendary yellow metal rarely deviated from this well-established norm. As the 1970s dawned, few were aware that the long-dormant gold trade was on the verge of one of the most astounding bull markets in U.S. financial history. In a few short years, a convergence of economic events like Nixon's decision to take the U.S. off the gold standard, the Carter-era energy crisis and runaway inflation sent gold prices through the roof. By 1980, an ounce of this most precious of metals would fetch a (then) all-time high of $850. In recent years, gold seems to be making something of a comeback.

The dollar's sudden decline, which began in 2002, has given new life to precious metals markets. In just a few short years—between 2005 and 2008—an ounce of gold surged from under $520 to well over $900. While the current deflationary crisis has put the brakes on the gold market somewhat, this popular inflation hedge is still fetching over $800 an ounce, and has outperformed most equities and major commodities (like oil). Gold's unexpected staying power seems to indicate a continued lack of confidence by investors in the dollar's long-term prospects. Many fear that the federal government's overheated stimulus spending and gargantuan debts won't be able to check the dollar's continued decline and foresee serious difficulties. If the markets are trending toward inflation, and the Consumer Price Index starts to climb, shifting some of your assets into gold is an excellent way to protect the value of your savings.

There is something psychologically comforting about knowing that you own something that is universally accepted and valued. As any economic historian will attest, during desperate economic times most stocks, bonds and even fiat currencies can be rendered worthless. Conversely, while the price of gold may fluctuate, you will never run the risk of being wiped out.

Gold can be purchased any number of ways. If you're averse to storing gold in your home and want to avoid the headache of opening up a safety deposit box, many gold investors rely on SPDR Gold Trust (GLD), an exchange traded fund (EFT) that allows you to purchase gold without the necessity or expense of actually taking it into your possession. Every share you buy is the equivalent of one-tenth of an ounce of gold with a small surcharge to cover the trust's operating expenses. The trust's web page can be found at www. spdrgoldshares.com/sites/us. The iShares Comex Gold Trust (IAU) is another ETF that offers consumers a reliable and convenient way to purchase gold. The company web page is at us.ishares.com. In light of the record losses incurred by most major stocks due to the economic crisis, both funds have performed remarkably well.

Some consumers are unwilling to trust a third party to safely store their assets, and would prefer to have direct possession of their gold investments. If you'd prefer something a bit more tangible, gold bullion coins like the American Eagle, Canadian Maple Leaf, Australian Nugget or South African Krugerrand are an effective way to store your gold. You can purchase many of these coins at most dealerships in your area, or you can look online at the American Precious Metals Exchange (apmex.com).

Many of the coins come in multiple weights that range from a fraction of an ounce to a full ounce, which means that consumers of all income levels can safeguard a portion of their assets by investing in gold. Should inflation run amok, your assets will not erode as most fiat currencies do during periods of financial instability. However, you will need to keep in mind that timing is important. If the economy starts trending toward inflation, akin to what transpired in the 1970s, many consumers could be priced out of the market.

While there are diehard precious metals enthusiasts who believe that buying gold is a worthwhile investment during any sort of economic downturn, should you invest in gold during a deflationary period? There is no easy answer. When there is deflation, the currency is in demand, and this will usually weaken enthusiasm for gold as a possible safe haven. However, at a time when real estate, stocks and other assets are increasingly risky, gold remains one of the safer forms of wealth, and has proven remarkably resilient to Depression 2.0 when compared to other types of investments. Moreover, if you truly believe inflation will rise, a deflationary period may prove to be the perfect time to enter the market at a reduced price.

Silver

FOR MANY OF THE REASONS WE MENTIONED ABOVE, SILVER OFFERS yet another conservative investment option. Like gold, silver languished at a steady price throughout much of the mid-20th century and then took off in the 1970s when stagflation crippled the U.S. economy. By the end of the 1970s, the price of silver would reach its zenith at just under $50 an ounce after spending decades in the $3–5 range. Although silver would face an intractable bear market for the next few decades, it seems to be climbing in value once again. Although you could buy an ounce of silver for just $5 in 2001, by 2008 the price had almost tripled. While the market has dropped off slightly, experts see ample room for continued growth.

The key issue is supply. At the dawn of the 20th century, the world was awash in silver. There were literally billions of ounces available. Today, much of the world's silver has been exhausted. Unlike gold, silver has a number of industrial applications in computers, defense technology, electronics, medicine and other fields. Indeed, according to a March 2007 analysis of the global silver supply published by *Marketwatch,* "The amount of silver above ground is projected to shrink to a critically low level in 2010."[2] Investment trends are also pointing toward a possible bull market for silver. In 2008, as part of its bullion program, the U.S. Mint sold an estimated 19,583,500 ounces of silver—an all-time high.[3]

The combined pressures of industrial demand, international jewelry markets and investors seeking a hedge against inflation could push silver to the forefront of the precious metals markets. Like gold, silver is a universally recognized commodity that will always possess value. If the predictions prove correct and the amount of available silver reaches a crisis point, silver may prove to be an increasingly attractive investment option. Like gold, silver has a few existing Exchange Traded Funds if you'd like to avoid taking physical possession of your silver purchases. You can invest in the iShares Silver Trust (SLV)—the company web page is at us.ishares.com. You can also purchase silver through the recently launched Powershares DB Silver Fund (DBS), at invescopowershares.com. Both funds took when the silver markets cooled off in response to the economic crisis, but have rebounded nicely.

Silver can also be obtained in a number of different forms. Because the federal government stopped making 90% silver coins in the mid-1960s, most coin dealers offer bags of "junk silver" which contain roughly $1,000 worth of pre-1965 nickels, dimes, quarters and half dollars. Although the coins are retailing for some $5,000 for half a bag and over $10,000 for a full bag, silver experts believe these outdated coins, which are often melted into bars to create silver bullion, will rise in value over time. In an absolute worst-case scenario, these coins could also prove to be an effective emergency currency in the event of a serious currency collapse of devaluation—so there's also a practical side to investing in outdated silver currency.

You should also pay attention to estate and garage sales in your area, as you might run across silver jewelry, candleholders and other items that can be purchased at a reduced price. If you'd like to purchase bars, rounds or coins made of silver, the American Precious Metals Exchange (APMEX) offers one of the better selections. However, you will need to keep in mind that shipping costs could be expensive if you plan on placing a large order.

While silver is an excellent store of value in an inflationary situation, whether or not to purchase silver in a deflationary scenario poses the same possible pitfalls we mentioned with gold. Since the current crisis unfolded, we've already seen a small decline in silver. However, like gold, should inflation materialize, you may find that silver prices will resume their upward trend, and it might be worthwhile to get into the market now.

Bonds

WHEN WE THINK OF CONSERVATIVE INVESTMENTS, THE IDEA OF PURchasing bonds immediately comes to mind. Bonds are basically a type of loan that must be repaid at a certain rate of interest. In essence, a bond is a glorified I.O.U. that can be issued by companies, municipalities, states and other entities seeking funding. Because they are rated in terms of risk and pay a slightly higher rate than most CD accounts, many consider bonds to be a safe, stable alternative to the often volatile stock market.

However, in a deflationary situation, bonds are anything but safe. Keep in mind that when a company defaults on its bonds, it's not simply a matter of getting stiffed on your interest payments—the bonds themselves will be worthless. During the last major deflation in the U.S—the Great Depression—a great many companies defaulted on their bonds, leaving investors with little more than worthless paper. In the middle of an economic crisis, it's a risky bet to think that a company will be able to pay its debts in the middle of a global credit crunch.

Government bonds are no less problematic in a deflationary scenario. Most states and municipalities are struggling and will find it hard to merely service existing debts. We could see a wave of defaults if the deflation drags on and tax revenues continue to slide. Perhaps the only exception is U.S. Treasury bonds. It is highly unlikely that the federal government will default, and the value of fixed payments tends to rise during a deflation—during the Great Depression the purchasing power of $100 rose to $135 in just five years—which is why treasuries are considered a popular deflation hedge.

Inflation isn't much better for bonds. When inflation takes off, any interest you may have earned on your investment will be effectively neutralized by the dollar's declining value. For example, if you were to purchase a $10,000 bond that earns five percent interest, should inflation shoot up to seven percent, any returns you make on your principal investment will be wiped away. This may explain why bonds did poorly during the 1970s, when consumers faced double-digit inflation.

If you've been paying attention to the financial media you've probably heard great things about Treasury Inflation Protected Securities (TIPS). These bonds are issued by the U.S. Treasury, and are designed to rise with the rate of inflation. The way it works, with each incremental rise in the Consumer Price Index your principal and interest payments will expand as well. The interest income on TIPS bonds are described as "real" yields because, unlike other bonds, your earnings will be guaranteed regardless of the current rate of inflation.

At first glance, TIPS and other inflation-protected bonds sound particularly tempting as a safe haven for your assets when inflation is high. Unfortunately, the Consumer Price Index has come under increasing scrutiny in recent years. Critics contend that the U.S. government no longer measures inflation the way it was calculated during the 1970s. The use of hedonic pricing formulas, geometric weighting and other dubious measures has many convinced that the federal government is using statistical sleight-of-hand to artificially lower the official rate of inflation.

Economist John Williams, who operates the Shadow Government Statistics web page (shadowstats.com), makes a very compelling case that inflation is significantly higher than the CPI indicates. Moreover, the government has every incentive to keep inflation rates low to limit payouts to TIPS holders and Social Security recipients whose earnings are adjusted each year for inflation. While the TIPS concept may seem attractive, until the CPI is a more reliable measure of inflation, if you gamble on inflation-protected securities your money will be tied up in a dubious proposition.

Real Estate

WHILE IT IS DIFFICULT TO SPECULATE WHAT THE FUTURE HOLDS FOR the nation's embattled real estate markets, the outlook appears anything but promising. In August 2008, Yale professor Robert Shiller, who helped devise the U.S. home pricing index, and is considered one of the nation's foremost real estate experts, predicted that American home prices will likely drop to "Depression-era" levels in the immediate future. In other words, we have yet to reach bottom. In 2008 alone, home prices were reduced by an estimated 20% in value, and we can expect at least another 10% reduction or more before prices begin to stabilize. Does this offer a possible safe haven for your cash? It all depends on your perspective.

In recent years, the financial media has promoted the notion that owning a home is an investment in and of itself. The prevailing belief is that if you buy a home, it will appreciate in value, and then you sell it at a significant profit. However, you need to keep in mind that the housing bubble of the early 21st century can largely be attributed to the Federal Reserve's reckless currency policy, poorly managed banks and the growth of mortgage-backed securities. History tells us that homes have rarely been perceived as money-making investments. In his book *Irrational Exuberance*, Shiller closely analyzed home prices from 1890 to the present and found that other than two brief upticks, real home prices overall have been flat or declining for the better part of the last century.[4] In other words, the surging home prices of the late 1990s and early 21st century were more a statistical aberration than any serious investment trend.

If you're willing to change your outlook and look at a home as a durable consumer good and store of value, then you might run across a bargain, especially as prices continue to fall for available homes. Although a deflationary period isn't exactly the best time to take on debt, and banks have become increasingly tight-fisted with home loans, if you feel you can handle the added expense for the foreseeable future, there are obvious benefits to owning your own property during difficult economic times. Your assets will be tied up in something of definite value that can provide you years of comfort and enjoyment. And, should the dollar go into a tailspin, you can look forward to repaying your loan with increasingly cheaper dollars. However, if you're looking to "flip" a home and double your money, you'll have to wait for another speculative bubble.

Stocks

THE MAJORITY OF US DON'T OWN SHARES OF STOCK IN THE TRADI-tional way. Instead, equities are purchased on our behalf through employee 401k pension plans. It's likely your retirement fund has taken a serious beating due to the current crisis. As of February 2009, most plans were down by 20% or more. Should you pull your money out? The overall consensus among financial advisors is to stay the course.

Retirement accounts are designed for the long term, and if you keep this in mind, a protracted bear market isn't an altogether bad thing from a big-picture perspective. Because stock prices have dropped, your contributions will actually buy more, and if the market rebounds you will have increased the size of your retirement portfolio at a reduced cost. However, you will need to ensure that your plan isn't being poorly managed. A new rating service called BrightScope has begun posting reviews of 401K plans online (brightscope.com) to see if your company plan is listed. If there is reason for concern, consider rolling over your current 401k into an alternate plan or Individual Retirement Account (IRA) more to your liking. Be sure to consult with a financial advisor or your company 401k manager to discuss your options.

When it comes to retirement accounts, age should be your foremost consideration. If you are close to retirement, you may not have the time to recoup your losses. However, if you decide that you simply can't watch your fund take any more losses, remember that cashing in your 401k can often result in a number of financial penalties. If you liquidate your account and are under the age of fifty-nine and a half, you will incur a 10% early withdrawal penalty. The proceeds from your fund will also be considered taxable income by the IRS. By the time you've paid your taxes and penalties, your distribution will be significantly reduced. Moreover, because many state employment agencies view these funds as a form of deferred salary, you may run into difficulties applying for unemployment should you lose your job. If you're older and concerned about your 401k, your best option is rolling over your plan into a better performing IRA or other type of qualified tax-deferred retirement plan better suited to your individual needs.

If you'd like to invest directly in the stock market, finding some relatively safe stocks in a deflationary situation won't be easy. In *Conquer the Crash*, a deflation survival guide, author Robert R. Prechter suggests investing in a short-selling mutual fund like the Prudent Bear Fund (BEARX) or the Comstock Capital Value Fund (CPCRX) to ride out a bear market. These kinds of managed portfolios generally take a majority short position on various stocks with a few long positions. However, it is worth pointing out that both of these funds, which did quite well through much of 2008, appear to have misread the market and lost significant value in the ensuing deflationary meltdown when inflation dropped and the dollar gained strength. While both funds have improved their performance, this kind of volatility shows that even market skeptics are having a tough time negotiating the rough waters of the current crisis. However, over the long term, perhaps these funds might prove to be one of the safer options available in a deflationary situation. If you'd like more information, the web page for the Prudent Bear Fund is at prudentbearfunds.com, and you can learn more about the Comstock Capital Value Fund at gabelli.com.

While an inflationary scenario poses its own hazards, at least there are a few avenues that may prove worthwhile. For one, if fuel prices once again dominate the headlines, petroleum is a key economic sector that will enjoy a renewed resilience. Oil interests performed well in the 1970s, and we can expect similar growth should we experience another round of spiraling fuel prices. Established companies like Exxon Mobile (XOM) and British Petroleum (BP) that are engaged in oil extraction, refining and the development of petroleum-based products are a pretty good bet should fuel scarcity become prevalent. As natural gas supplants oil in some critical areas, companies like Devon Energy (DVN) that produce both oil and natural gas are another good option. Oil service contractors like Schlumberger (SLB) that provide well discovery and project management services to oil companies should also do well.

If energy worries deepen, ETFs directly tied to fuel prices might provide a safe haven for your money. For example, if you invest in the United States Oil Fund (USO) and the price of crude rises, your shares will rise as well. Check the web page for more information: unitedstatesoilfund.com. The aforementioned Everbank is also offering a New World Energy Index CD, which is directly tethered to the currencies of three non-Middle Eastern countries that are awash in natural resources (Australia, Canada and Norway). The interest-earning accounts require a minimum investment of $20,000 and are available in three- and-six month terms. So long as energy remains an issue, this might prove to be a relatively conservative investment.

If you're a bit more forward-looking in your investment strategy, the emerging market for green technology is another area with possibly rich potential. Although still in its early stages, the clean energy sector will likely see continued growth as the world starts moving toward renewable power sources. One approach that might prove worthwhile is New Alternatives (NALFX), an equity fund that was founded in 1982 and is specifically geared toward long-term financial growth through investments in environmentally friendly technology. Although the fund has had its ups and downs, its overall performance is solid and offers potential as a quality investment. If you'd like more information about the fund, the company web page can be found at newalternativesfund. com.

If the dollar begins to stumble, you might consider investing in one of the Exchange Traded Funds that short the dollar. So long as the nation is plagued by budget and trade deficits, energy difficulties, massive debt, and prolonged and costly military deployments in the Middle East, betting against the dollar may prove to be a sound bet. The Power Shares U.S. Dollar Bearish Fund (UDN) takes a short position on the dollar versus a basket of foreign currencies that include the Euro, Japanese Yen, British Pound, Canadian Dollar, Swedish Krona and the Swiss Franc. The fund is managed by DB Commodity Services, and the company web page can be found at dbfunds.db.com. If you'd like to limit your exposure to shorting the dollar against the Euro, you might want to investigate the Euro Trust, an EFT issued by CurrencyShares (currencyshares.com).

The Informed Investor

WHILE WE'VE PROVIDED A FEW GENERAL SUGGESTIONS FOR INVEST-ing in the stock market, we make no claims to possessing any Nostradamus-like ability to foretell the future and urge the would-be investor to proceed with caution. As any student of human nature will attest, desperation tends to breed desperate acts. As stock market earnings tumble and dozens of firms go under or teeter on the brink of bankruptcy, we can expect to see a rise in Enron-type corporate fraud, Ponzi schemes, insider trading, embezzlement, fiduciary abuses, "pump and dump" scams and a number of other boardroom crimes and scandals. Before entrusting your hard-earned money to a broker or purchasing any shares of stock, take the time to closely investigate who you are dealing with.

You will need to be constantly vigilant and be prepared to ask some hard questions at the first sign of any underhanded dealings or misrepresentation. If you're simply not sure and don't want to risk your money in the stock market, there is nothing wrong with keeping your money in the bank or under a mat-tress until the market picks up—you'll probably end up doing better than many of Wall Street's leading investment banks.

We must also accept the fact that we can no longer rely on govern-ment economists and Wall Street experts to provide us with sound, unbiased information about the state of the economy. Each of us needs to pay closer attention to financial matters and, when making critical decisions, unplug from the Wall Street propaganda machine which hasn't served us well in the past. Fortunately, the internet has given birth to a well-established alternative financial media that wasn't available to investors in the past. While there is nothing wrong with perusing the *Wall Street Journal* or obtaining market data on Google Finance, be sure to explore some of the lesser-known outlets for more straightforward financial information and commentary. If you're unsure where to begin, we've included a small sampling of a few web pages that might prove helpful:

321 Gold (321gold.com): If you're interested in investing in precious metals, look no further than this page for information, daily quotes and commentary about the Federal Reserve and the PM market.

ASPO (aspo-usa.com): Even if you're the most determined Peak Oil skeptic, the Association for the Study of Peak Oil and Gas is a valuable online resource for energy-related news, commentary, and analysis.

The Daily Reckoning (dailyreckoning.com): Featuring the writings of acclaimed authors Bill Bonner, Addison Wiggin and other contrarian thinkers, the *Daily Reckoning* was far out in front in predicting the current crisis, and is an excellent source for acerbic financial commentary, market news and clear-headed discussions of the national debt, federal reserve policy energy issues, and other pertinent economic matters.

Euro Pacific Capital (europac.net): Known as "Dr. Doom" for his repeated warnings of impending economic disaster, author and financial analyst Peter Schiff has proven remarkably prescient in predicting the dot.com downfall and the collapse of the housing bubble. Euro Pacific Capital is his investment firm, and the webpage posts Schiff's frequent commentaries, resources for investors and frequently updated news items.

Global Guerillas (globalguerillas.typepad.com): Fourth Generation warfare, criminal networks, piracy and international terrorist groups have become a major source of economic disruption in the modern world. John Robb, the author of *Brave New War*, lends his unique perspective to daily news developments pertaining to decentralized insurgent groups and how they impact the global economy. He also posts information about how communities can become more economically resilient.

Investopedia (investopedia.com): If you're a raw beginner and don't have a good grasp of financial matters, this site, operated by *Forbes* magazine, has myriad helpful articles, tutorials and general information. The site even has a fantasy stock market game that you can use to hone your investing skills.

Prudent Bear (prudentbear.com): This is a great site for news and commentary that often goes against the prevailing Wall Street wisdom—and they are often invariably correct.

Schlumberger (slb.com): The web page for Schlumberger, the renowned oil services company, also offers a wide array of energy-related news, information and technical reports for investors seeking key information about emerging trends in the petroleum sector.

Seeking Alpha (seekingalpha.com): News, information, and interesting and often erudite commentary on both economics and finance. The site has excellent forums and the readers are generally well-informed and highly opinionated.

Shadow Government Statistics (shadowstats.com): John Williams publishes a monthly newsletter for subscribers ($175/year) and maintains a hard-hitting web page singularly devoted to exposing flaws in the federal government's economic reporting methods and providing consumers with realistic statistics about the current state of the economy. This is the type of information you will need at your fingertips during turbulent times.

At its most basic, investing is the art of deploying your assets wisely for the future. As we've mentioned, very few investors can emerge from a serious crisis with his or her money intact. If you break even, or lose a small sum, consider yourself lucky. Chances are you will have outperformed the majority of Wall Street's exalted investment gurus. If you prepare today, hopefully you can look forward to the future with a valuable financial cushion and a hopeful outlook toward the future. Good luck. •

Notes

1   "The Rise and (Almost) Fall of America's Banks," Associated Press, February 7, 2009.

2   Kerr, Kevin. "Silver May Shine Brightest Among Metals This Year," *Marketwatch*, March 15, 2007.

3   Zielinski, Michael. "Long Term Trend in Investment Demand for Silver," *Seeking Alpha*, February 6, 2009.

4   Shiller, Robert. *Irrational Exuberance*, (New York: Doubleday, 2005). p. 20.

CHAPTER 11

FUTURE SHIFT
THE REBOOTING OF
AMERICAN LIFE

Future Shift:
The Rebooting of American Life

THE MAJORITY OF THIS BOOK HAS BEEN FOCUSED ON THE PRACTICAL side of economic survival. Yet subsistence alone shouldn't be your only concern. For many of us, the greater challenge will be finding fulfillment at a time of diminishing expectations. The gut-wrenching economic convulsions of the present may one day be perceived as a historic turning point. In the near future, Americans will be forced to contemplate a whole new approach to how we live, work and spend our time. The transition will be far from painless, but those of us willing to creatively adapt needn't fear the future.

Humans are creatures of habit, and shifting over to new ways of doing things rarely comes easily. However, one needn't be a pessimist to sense that major changes are on the horizon. The fact is we may no longer have a choice. The consumer-driven lifestyle that has dominated our lives for the past quarter-century is simply no longer sustainable. As historian Andrew Bacevich has observed, the "prerequisites of the American way of life" have long "outstripped the means to satisfy them."[1] Global warming, fuel scarcity, our nation's financial woes and other pressing issues will force each of us to radically alter how we live.

We will also need to rethink the role of government in our lives. In the years to come, an increasingly greater percentage of our tax dollars will be redirected toward servicing the exorbitant debts our politicians have amassed over the past two decades. To maintain current operations, the federal government is already piling on $2 billion in debt each and every day. The National Center for Policy Analysis has stated that unless there is serious reform or additional tax revenues generated:

By 2012, the federal government will stop doing one in ten of the things it is doing now.

By 2020 the federal government will cease doing one in four.

By 2030, the federal government won't be able to perform half of the services it currently provides.[2]

The day has long since passed when we could expect our nation's dysfunctional political class to look after our interests. We will need to become more resilient, self-sufficient and better prepared. Adaptability and the ability to thrive amidst diversity are two of the most vital assets in our evolutionary tool kit. We can take comfort in the fact that each of us has the innate ability to transcend difficult circumstances and live rewarding, purposeful lives. Now might be a good time to take a long, hard look at what you consider important. Perhaps there's a more sustainable path to a more satisfying life. Should you have any lingering doubts, let's take a closer look at where our consumer obsessions have led us.

A Nation of Shoppers

MEET KRISTINE ROGERS, AN ADDICT. THE SUBURBAN MOTHER OF FOUR isn't ashamed to admit her costly habit drove her family deeply into debt. However, her unsavory life of excess wasn't triggered by any sordid, drug-fueled high, but by a children's clothing manufacturer known as Gymboree. Over a frantic two-year period, her obsession with outfitting her children in every possible Gymboree design and color combination escalated to a $400-per week shopping habit that entailed spending eight hours on the Internet each and every day looking for bargains and hard-to-find items. "Online, it felt like Monopoly money," she later told *Money* magazine. "I'd get a rush, a physical high," she added. "It got so bad that just thinking about shopping, I'd start shaking."[3] By the time Rogers figured out that she might have a problem, she'd run through $50,000, and her children's closets were stuffed beyond capacity.

She isn't alone. You might say there's a little bit of Kristine Rogers in each of us. Statistics indicate that approximately 8% of the population is seriously addicted to impulse buying, and there are probably just as many borderline cases—but they simply haven't maxed out their credit cards yet.[4] Here's the interesting thing: We rarely hear our politicians engaging in any sanctimonious finger-wagging about spendthrift shoppers. You might call it the respectable addiction. While our entire economy is being kept afloat by consumer spending, materialism has become something akin to a national imperative, a sort of credit-fueled panacea for whatever ails us. Who can forget a recent president's exhortation that Americans go shopping in the aftermath of the worst terrorist attack on American soil in history? Or as a former Federal Reserve governor once explained, "If we all join hands and go buy a new SUV, everything will be all right."[5]

When we aren't being prompted by our politicians to march in lockstep to the nearest megamall, we're being bombarded each and every day with literally hundreds of slickly-produced, highly persuasive pitches for myriad products and services that we usually don't even need. In the popular mind, advertising offers us a direct link to the so-called "good life": a conflict-free existence where attractive, intelligent and perpetually-grinning consumers have achieved supreme bliss through buying everything from the right oven cleaner to the newest model SUV. While few of us believe that we make our choices at the promptings of Madison Avenue behavioral specialists, we have on a certain level internalized the underlying message that our state of happiness is directly tied to how many luxury goods we own. Unfortunately, this fanciful alternate reality has taken a decisive toll on the quality of life in America.

The Price of Profligacy

WHEN WE LOOK AT THE SHEER SCOPE OF HOW MUCH DEBT WE HAVE accumulated in such a short time, there is simply no historical precedent. In 1975, as Americans struggled with a severe recession and soaring unemployment, the ratio of outstanding household debt to disposable income was 62%. Today, that number has surged to over 120%, while savings are still at record lows.[6] When we include unpaid mortgages, 2008 Federal Reserve estimates indicate that American families have absorbed a gargantuan debt load that now exceeds $2 trillion.[7] When we deal with these kinds of large numbers, it's easy to forget that there is a direct human cost to our material obsessions. In an age when financial pressures account for the majority of divorces in the U.S., we could be looking at an epidemic of broken homes. Moreover, many individuals may have to put off retirement due to the being burdened with these kinds of pressing debts—and the young may not enjoy the same benefits enjoyed by previous generations.

However, our financial woes are only the tip of the iceberg. Let's take a cursory look at one of our most precious commodities: our time. According to Take Back Our Time, a non-profit dedicated to ending the nation's "workaholic, time-rushed culture," the average American today works one month (160 hours) more than they did in 1976.[8] Indeed, just 14% of American workers take a vacation of two weeks or longer.[9] All too often, consumer debt has an insidious ratcheting effect: the more we owe, the more it ramps up pressure to work longer hours and earn more money. Thus, it is unsurprising that many employees simply can't say no to additional hours, unscheduled overtime, cancelled vacations and other workplace demands on their limited free time.

In previous years, absenteeism used to be a frequent complaint of corporate managers: someone was always calling in sick to nurse a hangover, go to a ball game or simply enjoy a bit of much-needed downtime. Today, the inverse is true: the new threat is called "presenteeism." Human resources managers are growing alarmed about workplace illnesses spread by feverish, coughing and sneezing employees who simply can't afford to take a day off. As over 40% of American workers have no recourse to paid sick time, many have little choice but to keep on working when sick—even if it means running the risk of infecting co-workers.[10]

The fact is, a lot of us simply can't afford to lose out on a day's pay. When you're barely keeping your head above water and struggling with a burdensome mortgage, credit card debt or blowing all your disposable income at the mall, a reduced paycheck simply isn't an option. Yet this frenetic, treadmill-like pace is only making our problems worse. Indeed, Americans report feeling anxiety and depression far more than Europeans, and this may have a great deal to do with our overall lack of free time.

Our outsized appetites have even impacted how we choose to live. In the 1950s, when families were larger and people were on average far happier than they are today, the average home size was a mere 950 square feet. Today, the norm is well over 2,000 feet, and we still don't have enough space to hold all of our cherished "stuff." Renting out storage units is now a $22 billion-a-year industry.[11] Meanwhile, the fuel-efficient compact cars of the '70s and '80s have been replaced on America's highways by gas-guzzling SUVs, the dream car of every mall shopper. Yet all of these possessions have left many of us overworked, stressed out and fearful about the future.

Happiness Unbound

SO WHY DO SO MANY AMERICANS FEEL SO EMPTY WHILE SURROUNDED by so much material abundance? What exactly is the so-called "good life"? These questions are far from insignificant. Our ability to maintain a positive, hopeful outlook will have a direct bearing on how we contend with our nation's economic difficulties and the changes on the horizon. Fortunately, in recent years the mental health establishment has been focusing more on the under-lying psychology of what makes us happy. Over the past decade, researchers working in the nascent field of positive psychology have conducted a number of studies dedicated to unlocking this elusive state of mind. These initial findings have destroyed a number of long-cherished beliefs and brought the nature of human contentment into sharper focus.

The long-held belief that purchasing power dictates happiness can be traced back to the rise of behavioral psychology in the mid-20th century. The behavioral theorists who held sway in the Cold War era believed that our innate drive to acquire material possessions was a Darwinian survival mechanism encoded in our DNA. The wealthier we became, the behavioralists believed, the more likely we would attract a superior mate and produce healthy, intelligent offspring. Thus, it was concluded that we were simply hardwired to feel happiness when we had material wealth, and sadness when we didn't—our survival depended on it. This questionable model of human behavior would go on to shape advertising for decades to come. However, what we know today about human happiness challenges this long-held belief.

While it is commonly believed that the epitome of fulfillment is to be wealthy, young and intelligent, research reveals a far more complex picture. The super-rich aren't any happier than the rest of us, older people tend to be more content than the young and there is no direct correlation between one's IQ and ability to be happy. Perhaps our greatest mistake is confusing pleasure and happiness. While the momentary joys we may derive from sex, chocolate, television or a shopping trip may add sparkle to our lives, these activities are no substitute for authentic, lasting happiness. Martin Seligman, who is considered the intellectual father of positive psychology, contends that our sense of well-being rests upon three specific criteria: engagement, meaning and pleasure. "The belief that we can rely on shortcuts to happiness, joy, rapture, comfort and ecstasy," he writes, "leads to legions of people who in the middle of great wealth are starving spiritually."[12]

What he means by engagement is simply that individuals who possess deeper and more meaningful connections to their families, friends, co-workers and neighbors tend to be more satisfied with their lives. Seligman points to a 2002 study he conducted at the University of Illinois with his colleague Edward Diener. The two scholars found that the most common attribute among the small percentage of students who enjoyed a high level of happiness was a strong commitment to spending time with friends and family.[13]

Yet this isn't the whole picture either. Humans also require an overall sense of purpose to their lives. When we cannot derive any sort of meaning from our daily existence, it is often difficult to feel hopeful about the future, much less the present. For example, a penniless street artist who believes he is contributing to his country's cultural betterment or pursuing his artistic vision may be happier and better adjusted than a well-to-do attorney who hates the legal profession.

The search for meaning in our lives also has a great deal to do with how we deploy our strengths and aptitudes. When these skills aren't given a creative outlet either in our work or our spare time, life begins to lose its luster. A perfect example of how we can derive happiness from our strengths is the concept of *flow*. The term was first coined by psychologist Mihaly Csikszentmihalyi roughly two decades ago to denote the "optimal psychological experience."

Flow experiences are those memorable (and often life-changing) moments when every atom of our existence is dedicated to a particular task to the point where self-consciousness evaporates and time literally stands still. Think of a mountaineer scaling a particularly challenging rock face, a novelist working through an inspired passage or a parent successfully teaching his or her child to walk for the first time. When we have these exhilarating experiences, we feel like we are masters of our own fate and that life's great challenges can be overcome. Above all else, we seem to obtain these singular moments when we are exercising our signature strengths.

Think about the last time you had a serious flow experience. It probably didn't involve keying in your PIN number at a mall cash register or jockeying for a parking space outside Best Buy. Indeed, we can see that happiness and consumerism are often at odds with one another. For far too long we have substituted the ephemeral pleasures of buying "stuff" for a more lasting happiness. However, we can take great comfort in the fact that even if we must accept a reduced standard of living, so long as our basic needs are met, there is nothing stopping us from enjoying our lives to the fullest. In fact, there is already a small but growing minority of Americans who have already come to this important realization.

Where Consumer Culture Wanes and Real Life Begins

YOU MIGHT SAY LAURA GARDINER IS SOMETHING OF A CULTURAL mutant. The Chicago resident works part-time at a job she loves, isn't in debt, avoids shopping malls and spends her free time in more fruitful pursuits like volunteering for causes that she deeply cares about. Although she's still in her twenties, she has already paid off her student loans and resides with eight other tenants in a three-apartment housing unit operated by the Allium Collective, an activist group dedicated to bettering the planet by embracing simpler, more energy-efficient lifestyles. While she admits to the infrequent craving for eating at her favorite local restaurants, Gardiner has turned the prevailing wisdom on its head and carved out a meaningful life for herself on her own terms and without all the consumerist baggage. Here's the best part: unlike the rest of us, she's not worried about what's going to happen to the economy or how she will cope with financial disaster. It's simply not an issue. "I have the resources to survive," she told *Time Out Chicago* in a December 2008 interview. "Should everything fall apart, I have a support network."[14]

Gardiner offers a good example of how we can unshackle ourselves from the borrow-and-spend lifestyle and still live life to the fullest. Laura is part of a small but growing "voluntary simplicity" movement that may take on a new relevance as Americans rediscover the art of frugal living. However, saving money and living on less is only a part of the simplicity concept, as it is also rooted in the belief that we can live more fulfilling lives when we rid ourselves of the time-wasting complications that materialism brings into our lives.

Many who have scaled back their lifestyles have come to the realization that working less and having fewer possessions has actually improved every facet of their lives. When you're not overworked, fretting over bills or spending all your time buying things on the internet or at the mall, you have more time to spend with friends, family and neighbors. When you're only focused on basic necessities, you simply don't worry anymore about your prized new laptop crashing or the new SUV getting scratched. Stepping off the consumer treadmill can also be a launching point for self-growth, as you can devote more time to relationships, exercising more, catching up on your reading and the creative pursuits you've long wanted to explore but never had the time to.

Mention the word "frugal," and most of us will think "tightwad" or "miser." However, no one is telling you to live like a Trappist monk. Indeed, there is nothing wrong with enhancing your life with the occasional luxury or the modern conveniences that add a spark to our lives. However, the key is striking a balance between our material wants and the innumerable pleasures that we often neglect in the mad scramble to acquire more possessions. Those who embrace simpler lives would simply prefer to eat a nutritious, low-cost meal at home with friends and family than eat at an overpriced restaurant chain. If they get the urge to see a movie, they'd rather bicycle to the library and rent a DVD for free than drive to the megamall and incur the added expense of paying for gas, parking, tickets and refreshments.

Why buy something brand new that can be purchased used or repaired? This kind of self-reliance is highly valued among simplicity adherents. Growing your own fruits and vegetables, learning how to do your own home and auto repairs, and living off-grid are examples of how these individuals are creating a more authentic lifestyle that will make them particularly resilient during turbulent economic times. Take a good, long look at how you allocate your time each day. Are you giving yourself adequate space to unwind? Are you spending your evenings glued to the television set or computer? Is there a hobby, activity or pastime you used to really enjoy doing that you've dropped because you simply don't have the time? Every spare moment you have on this earth is crucial—try to think of ways you can add more joy to your life without spending money.

Work to Live or Live to Work?

ONE OF THE MOST INTERESTING FACETS OF THE SIMPLICITY MOVE-ment is how these individuals are changing the way Americans perceive work. It is well worth remembering that there were futurists in the late 1960s who predicted that advanced automation and labor-saving devices would reduce the American work week to a mere fourteen to twenty hours by the year 2000. Unfortunately, at some point we seem to have taken a wrong turn. And we don't enjoy the same job security and benefits that once existed for previous generations. Perhaps you're one of the fortunate ones who truly enjoys your work, and finds it both challenging and meaningful. However, far too many of us are simply going through the motions to pay the bills. If you're unhappy with your current situation, and feel your skills are being wasted in performing mindless drudgery, maybe it's time to rethink how you perceive work.

When you disconnect from the rat race and radically lower your standard of living, the suffocating pressures to earn more money suddenly vanish. Simplicity advocates call it "breaking the link between work and wages." Instead of allowing your monetary needs to dictate what you do for a living, you have the option of choosing something that will best utilize your skills and provide you with a creative, worthwhile outlet for your time. This doesn't mean slacking, either. Some people who have "downsized" have started their own businesses and put in even longer hours, but they are often doing something they truly enjoy.

Laura Gardiner, who we mentioned earlier, is a perfect example. Her frugal lifestyle allows her to make ends meet with a part-time teaching position that she enjoys. The rest of her time is her own. She has no outstanding debts and affordable rent, and thus few worries. While this might not be the most opportune time to leave your job and embark on a new career or small business, especially when there is widespread unemployment, it's still an important first step to begin to view work as something beneficial to your life and not a strict necessity. Indeed, you may still find employment opportunities that you never knew existed when you're no longer contending with an economic straitjacket.

So how do you begin? The transition won't be easy, and may require keeping your current position, going back to school, pursuing job training or taking a few survival jobs until you've found your niche. The more you reduce your reliance on credit, limit your outgoing cash flow and increase your savings, the more breathing room you will have to pursue more challenging job opportunities. "Downshifters," as they like to call themselves, advise people seeking a change of work to do what they call a "SWOT analysis"—i.e., analyze your strengths, weaknesses, opportunities and threat factors, and try to assemble a realistic list of job or entrepreneurial possibilities. If you're serious about changing your life, you may also need to rethink your current mode of living.

Downsize Your Lifespace

MAYBE THIS SOUNDS LIKE YOUR PLACE: THE FRONT DOOR CAN HARDLY close because of the stacks of unread magazines, newspapers and junk mail piled near the entrance. The living room coffee table is buckling under the weight of various items of bric-a-brac, remote controls, books, DVDs, used dishes and other random objects. The bedroom is even worse. Piles of clothes, both clean and freshly laundered, take up most of the available floor space. The bed itself has become a sort of de facto hanger with jackets, blankets, robes and other items draped across the bedposts. The closets are stuffed beyond capacity. The storage space in the garage area is so filled with exercise equipment, rarely-used tools and other possessions that slamming the door is enough to set off an avalanche.

There's a reason why Americans are requiring bigger and bigger lodgings: We simply can't fit all of our belongings into a traditional apartment or small-sized home. A severely cluttered home or apartment isn't just a safety issue—it can become a mental health issue over time as well. "People's homes are a reflection of their lives," says Peter Walsh, a psychologist who specializes in helping people organize their lives. "It's no accident that people have a huge weight problem in this country, and clutter is the same thing. Homes are an orgy of consumption."[15]

Like modern-day hunter-gatherer tribes, literally millions of American families have amassed so much stuff that their homes come closer to resembling a deranged modern art display than a suitable place to live. Some have become so ashamed at how cluttered and disorderly their homes have become that they no longer feel comfortable inviting friends, neighbors or family over to visit. In essence, they are buying themselves into hermetic isolation.

The disorganized sprawl also takes a heavy financial toll. The more stuff we acquire, the more likely it is that we will have to pay additional rent or a costlier mortgage because we can't fit all of our possessions into a cozy one-bedroom apartment or smaller-sized home. There is also the added expense of renting a storage unit when you run out of places to stash your hoard of possessions. Clutter is also mentally and physically exhausting. Even the simplest household chores can take hours when you can never find anything. However, what is most insidious about excessive clutter is that it can often turn your home into a prison. At a time of great economic uncertainty, flexibility is important. Relocating at a moment's notice to pursue a job or move into a cheaper place is virtually impossible when you're terrified at the thought of even trying to organize and pack up your numerous belongings. It doesn't have to be this way.

If you're inundated with clutter, your life will be that much harder during difficult economic times, and you'll be that much more resistant to make any significant changes to your lifestyle. Perhaps it's time to liberate your household and start fresh. If you get your possessions under control, you'll find that your day-to-day life won't seem as unmanageable, that it becomes easier to concentrate and that you will be open to any number of alternative housing options and employment possibilities. If you're having trouble getting started, try following some of the suggestions we've included below:

Start a "Never Used" Pile: We all have possessions that we rarely use, but we've convinced ourselves that we simply can't do without them. While there are certain items that fall into this category that you'll want to keep, like a first aid kit, a flashlight or tools, there are other possessions that are simply taking up space. Start a pile of your belongings that you've never once used. Chances are, the majority of these items are simply taking up space. Have a garage sale and sell them, throw them out, barter them or donate them to charity. You'll be glad you did.

The "Wait and See" Box: Some of your purchases may have only been used once or twice, and you're simply not sure whether to throw them out. Create a "Wait and See" box and fill it with any objects you might not be sure about. Mark the date each item was placed in the box. Anything that's been in the box for six months or more that hasn't been used has to go.

Fifteen Minutes: One of the biggest obstacles to getting rid of excess clutter is that it is such a daunting task. The minute we start to envision all the work the process entails, it's all too easy to put it off for another day. Try clearing up your home in small increments. Spend fifteen to twenty minutes each day decluttering, and you'll soon begin to see a difference. You can also try reducing the clutter in just one small section of your home or apartment each day, and then continue enlarging your clutter-free zone.

Another Set of Eyes: Some possessions have a great deal of sentimental value to us, but to a disinterested onlooker, these treasured mementos are simply garbage. Keeping a collection of over 700 Star Wars action figures or twenty-seven copies of that newspaper edition that printed your letter to the editor might make sense to you, but to a friend or relative these personal keepsakes are just taking up space. Invite someone over who doesn't have the same emotional attachment to your possessions to help with your decluttering efforts. It might result in some hurt feelings, but in the end, you'll get some much-needed perspective.

Set Guidelines: Let's assume you've completely cleared up your apartment and that it's now a well-organized living space. Unfortunately, after a few mall trips, a spending spree at the used bookstore, and several days of accumulated junk mail, you're suddenly falling into the same trap. Try to create some ground rules for yourself that will inhibit any further hoarding. For example, make a rule that for every new possession you bring into your home or apartment, you have to cast away two items you currently own.

Adapting and Thriving

CASTING ASIDE YOUR CURRENT LIFESTYLE AND PURSUING A MORE scaled-down existence won't happen overnight. Old habits often die hard. Nevertheless, you must always remember that resiliency breeds confidence. Once you've taken the first tentative step toward greater self-sufficiency, you may find that many of your fears were largely illusory. There is no denying that Depression 2.0 will impact each of us in both small and significant ways. Yet we must keep in mind that the economic dislocations of the present day are but a symptom of the major changes that are looming on the horizon.

We often forget that the "Green Revolution" of the late 20th century that allowed American food production to reach unheard-of levels was largely powered by cheap fuel. Modern fertilizers rely on an abundant and inexpensive source of natural gas. Irrigation systems require fossil fuels, and the majority of pesticides are derived from petroleum. Should fuel scarcity become a permanent fixture in American life or should global petroleum markets become destabilized, America's legendary abundance may become a relic of a bygone era. Yet oil isn't the only consideration. The onset of global warming will only further complicate the picture.

Important agricultural regions like China and Argentina have both experienced severe droughts that have greatly impacted food production. Indeed, in Australia lack of rainfall has been a recurring problem since 2004. According to a recent report, "The drought has been so severe that rivers stopped flowing, lakes turned toxic and farmers abandoned their land in frustration."[16] And American isn't immune. In California, a reduction in the Northern Sierra snowpack has triggered a serious water shortage and one of the state's worst droughts. Texas, Florida and Georgia are also contending with inadequate rainfall and water shortages, which will greatly impact agricultural efforts. Should the crisis spread, we could witness food shortages.

Expecting top-heavy government bureaucracies to address complex problems of this magnitude may no longer be an option. However, the growth and emergence of resilient communities dedicated to sustainable living offer a hopeful alternative. The advent of community and backyard gardening initiatives, citizen preparedness efforts, alternative currencies, co-housing arrangements, bartering clubs, ecovillages and other innovations offer a promising glimpse into our post-carbon future. Indeed, thanks to advanced social networking technology, connecting with like-minded individuals and organizations in your area has never been easier.

The day may come when each of us will play a larger role in the economic life of our communities. We may find ourselves supporting local farms through Community Supported Agriculture (CSA) programs, lending our skills to neighborhood time banks, bartering our homegrown produce at farmers' markets, and spending our money with alternative currencies as opposed to inflated greenbacks. Indeed, these small-scale endeavors may one day supplant the traditional marketplace and provide critical goods and services at a time when credit is scarce and the currency is unstable.

Historically, Americans are a resilient people. Throughout our nation's history we have repeatedly shown our ability to pick up and rebuild in the face of wars, economic depressions, and countless tests of our national will. When we put our differences aside, work together, and deploy our creative talents, there is no limit to what we can accomplish. Depression 2.0 and the ensuing challenges of the 21st century may loom large in the public imagination. Nevertheless, we needn't fear the future so long as we possess the resolve and the imagination to squarely face what lies ahead. •

Notes

1   Bacevich, Andrew. "Appetite for Destruction," *American Conservative*, September 2008.

2   "Expect Much Less Government," National Center for Policy Analysis, *Daily Policy Digest*, November 11, 2008.

3   Caplin, Joan. "Confessions of a Compulsive Shopper," *Money*, November 4, 2005.

4   Ibid.

5   McTeer, Robert. Remarks before the Richardson Chamber of Commerce, February 2001.

6   Foster, John Bellamy. "The Household Debt Bubble," *Monthly Review*, May 2006.

7   Federal Reserve Board. "G29 Release: Consumer Debt: September 2008," November 7, 2008.

8   Hunsinger, Dana. "Getting Away Shouldn't Be Just for the Birds," *Indianapolis Star*, November 3, 2008.

9   Ibid.

10 Selvin, Molly. "Go Ahead, Call in Sick," *Los Angeles Times*, November 29, 2005.

11 Brown, Martin John. "Too Much Stuff! America's New Love Affair With Self-Storage," *Alternet*, June 4.

12 Seligman, Martin. *Authentic Happiness*, (Free Press: New York, 2002).

13 Wallis, Claudia. "The New Science of Happiness," *Time*, January 9, 2009.

14 Heisler, Steve. "Footloose and Financial Responsibility Free," *Time Out Chicago*, December 4–10, 2009.

15 "America's Orgy of Consumption," *Associated Press*, October 22, 2005.

16 deCarbonnel, Eric. "Catastrophic Fall in 2009 Global Food Production," *The Market Oracle*, February 9, 2009.

FROM

process self-reliance series

Preparedness Now!
An Emergency Survival Guide for
Civilians and Their Families
BY ATON EDWARDS

*"Aton Edwards is a man with the perfect
skills for our troubled times."* —BBC Radio

336 pages • illustrated
ISBN 978-0976082255 • $15.95

Getting Out
Your Guide to Leaving America
BY MARK EHRMAN

*"Ehrman's well-designed, all-encompassing
guidebook provides detailed instructions
for fleeing 'before America comes crashing
down upon you.'"* —Publishers Weekly

340 pages • illustrated
ISBN 978-0976082279 • $16.95

The Urban Homestead
Your Guide to Self-Sufficient Living
in the Heart of the City
BY KELLY COYNE AND ERIK KNUTZEN

*"This book is a one-stop shop about how to
be a homesteader when you live in the city.
It's a great read and is a must-have addition
to your reference library."* —Groovy Green

308 pages • illustrated
ISBN 978-1934170014 • $16.95

processmediainc.com